Good Homes magazine

D0247701

101 LIVING ROOMS

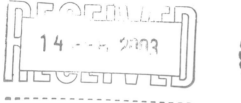

Published by BBC Worldwide Ltd
Woodlands
80 Wood Lane
London W12 0TT

First published 2002
Copyright © BBC Worldwide 2002
All photographs © *BBC Good Homes
magazine* 2002

ISBN 0 563 53438 9

Edited by Alison Willmott

Commissioning Editor: Nicky Copeland
Project Editors: Rhianwen Bailey and
Sarah Lavelle
Book Design: Claire Wood
Design Manager: Lisa Pettibone

Set in Amasis MT, ITC Officina Sans,
New Baskerville
Printed and bound in France by
Imprimerie Pollina s.a. - L86915
Colour origination by
Kestrel Digital Colour, Chelmsford

Good Homes magazine

101 LIVING ROOMS
STYLISH ROOM SOLUTIONS

Julie Savill

CONTENTS

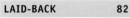

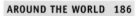

INTRODUCTION

There's a romantic notion that the kitchen is the heart of the home, the place where people get together, but if your kitchen is anything like the average you'll be lucky if there's enough space for a breakfast bar, let alone a Waltons-style clan gathering. Instead, for most people, the social area of the house is, of course, the living room. Relaxing evenings in front of the TV, games with the kids, drinks with a few mates – whatever activities your home life includes they happen here. All that activity is bound to take its toll and as a result this most public room in the house is the one that gets decorated most often.

There's a strong temptation to put on a plain face in a room that's open to this much scrutiny, to play safe with pale schemes that won't frighten the neighbours. But why worry about what they think? This room is, after all, yours and you should be decorating it to please yourself and suit your family. Practical reasoning is behind many a colour scheme and it's easy to see that with pets or kids in the house a barely there cream room might seem difficult to maintain. But with the latest washable matt emulsions for walls, forgiving blonde wood laminates for the floor and whip-off-and-wash covers on sofas it doesn't seem so distant a dream.

So, if you know your own mind colourwise and purple is what does it for you, bring it on. Or if whiter than white lights up your life, just do it. If, however, you need a nudge out of your old safe-is-best colour rut, this book is just the thing. Inspiration is all around us on TV, in magazines and in other people's houses, but when you're ready to redecorate what's needed is a deluge of ideas to pick and choose from, to copy exactly or to set your imagination spinning with your own plans and ideas. In this book you'll find all the ideas you need for living rooms in styles ranging from classic to contemporary, laid-back to budget, each explained from top to bottom so you can re-create the looks.

Julie Savill, Editor
BBC Good Homes magazine

The look: With an air of smart sophistication that would suit a city apartment, this room combines clean modern lines with fashionable dark wood, leather and tactile materials.

Colour: A neutral palette smartens up its act when it includes significant amounts of black or deep brown. The beige on the walls bridges the gap between the dark tones of the flooring, furniture and curtains and the cool creams of the rug and sofa. Touches of shine add high-tech glamour – metallic-effect paper covers the left wall.

Furniture: Modern designs with clean lines are essential for this look. Search the high street for designer-style furniture at budget prices. Cream sofas are a popular choice nowadays, so can be picked up relatively cheaply. Leather adds a feeling of luxury and sophistication – get the look for less with

a pair of inexpensive office chairs and a cube covered in fake leather.

Window: Although the fashion is for light, sheer window dressings, adding a coloured drape can help to frame and define your window. This one introduces a vertical dash of chocolate brown to balance the dark shades near floor level. The window treatments also add pattern – the brown curtain features a lively swirl design, while square motifs embellish the broad expanse of the white voile panel.

Accessories: Mirrors with silver-leaf frames add their glimmer to the metallic detailing in the room. Their circular shape echoes the swirl designs on the curtains. Use cushions to introduce more pattern, as well as tactile texture, with knitted and suede-effect fabrics. A flokati rug adds deep-pile comfort to the wooden floor.

The look: If you've played it safe with go-with-anything upholstery, the world of colour is wide open to you. Try teaming warm naturals with an aqua blue that's as refreshing as a dip in the sea.

Colour: Teaming bright aqua with mellow wood tones strikes a comfortable balance between warm and cool. Base your scheme on glowing natural colours, blending browns, creams and taupes in furniture and flooring, then temper the heat with a mid-tone blue on the walls. The silver-painted screen and table complement the coolness of the blue, while accents of yellow and orange brighten up the naturals.

Furniture: A screen is a stylish means of hiding clutter or dividing a room. This simple design is easy to make by hinging together three or four pieces of 50 x 200cm MDF. It is decorated with metallic silver paint and squares of silver leaf. The small side table is painted to match, introducing a high-tech glimmer to contrast with the natural tones of the wooden furniture and the soft texture of the suede-effect sofa cover.

Window: A Venetian blind is a versatile window treatment which allows you total control over light levels as the slats can be adjusted in varying degrees. Choose a wooden blind to complement a natural scheme.

Accessories: A picture is not only decorative in its own right but also adds accent colour – this Modigliani print echoes the reds and yellows of the cushions. The smooth surfaces of the wooden accessories highlight the beauty of their grain, which enriches the scheme with further natural tone and texture.

CONTEMPORARY

The look: A neutral scheme is rescued from plainness by two-colour tonal patterns, which add eye-catching detail yet are subtle enough to suit its soothing simplicity. The monochrome palette evokes an air of Japanese minimalism which is enhanced by the use of oriental-style furniture.

Colour: For a calming contemporary look, pick a limited palette of neutrals for both patterns and plains, using shades that are close in tone. Decorating the walls with a mid-tone such as taupe gives a more relaxing look than white or cream; a pale carpet lightens the effect. Navy blue is a softer alternative to black for a monochrome scheme, and including a selection of lighter but muted shades of blue helps to give the look a lift.

Pattern: At first glance this scheme might appear to be a homage to flat neutrals. But look closer and you'll see that the sofa is covered with a taupe and cream print and the foreground wall is papered with a script design on a subtle blue background. The bolder designs of the cushions and throw add further interest. Prints in one colour plus cream can be as calming and easy on the eye as plains, and are ideal for perking up a neutral scheme. Textured furnishings such as the waffle-weave carpet also introduce an element of pattern.

Furniture: Wooden furniture adds its own colour; here dark brown pieces strengthen the scheme with their deeper hues, while the orange-toned chair and coffee table add a warmer feel. Oriental furniture in dark wood and bamboo is now widely available and looks perfectly at home in simply styled contemporary interiors.

LIVING ROOM TIP
Cushions are great for adding pattern or colour in small amounts. They don't need much fabric, so search remnant bins in furnishing stores for offcuts at discount prices. This is an especially good idea if your scheme demands luxurious materials that are usually highly priced

The look: With French doors opening onto a balcony and a leafy view through the panes, this living room seeks to bring the garden indoors. Light linen blinds ensure that sunlight flows in unhindered, while natural materials and colours mirror bark and bough.

Colour: Rugged seagrass matting lays the foundation for a natural palette, which continues with the soft browns and tans of the chairs and the woven texture of the wicker tray. Green cushions and accessories echo the colours of spring leaves, while dashes of dark blue and tangerine sharpen the look with bolder accents. Plain white walls appear to fade into the background, minimizing the barrier between interior and garden while maximizing the airiness within the room.

Window: Simple Roman blinds provide shade from strong sunlight when needed, but otherwise pleat up neatly out of the way to let the view speak for itself. Their white linen blends with the surrounding walls and woodwork, and is fine enough to diffuse light without blocking it.

Furniture: A leather armchair and a sofa covered in brown Indian cotton ease into the natural scheme. Folding garden chairs emphasize the indoor-outdoor idea and can be taken out onto the balcony.

Shelf: The room has no fireplace but a large MDF mantelshelf has been built to create a focal point and display space. The enormous mirror resting on top helps to enhance the feeling of space by reflecting light.

LIVING ROOM TIP
Natural-fibre floorcoverings, such as seagrass, jute and coir, have attractive textured surfaces and are extremely hard-wearing. Some are difficult to keep clean as food spills easily become ingrained, but seagrass matting is naturally stain resistant

The look: Lighten up with clear, contemporary colours and floaty window dressings. Layered fabrics make play with a harmonious mix of blues, greens and lilacs for a refreshing atmosphere.

Colour: The patterned curtains form the starting point for this scheme, with the azure wall colour and the lilac of the sheer panel both picked out from its design. The colourwashed effect of the pattern and the translucence of the chiffon dilute the strength of the curtain colours, giving them a watery quality. Against this background, the solid turquoise of the chair makes it stand out, drawing attention to its shape. The cream throw and beige carpet provide a natural contrast.

Window: Layered curtains are both fashionable and practical. A sheer panel can remain drawn by day to shut out prying eyes without darkening the room. Light filters freely through super-fine chiffon or voile, which now come in many colours. If you want a more dressed look or need greater privacy in the evening, a double curtain pole lets you hang a second drape; this one is made of cotton. Headings have never been simpler – for a pretty look, top your curtain with pairs of narrow fabric strips and tie to the rings of your pole.

Furniture: A single piece of stunning furniture can make all the difference to your scheme. With the three-piece suite no longer in fashion, chairs can add individual style, so if budget restrictions force you to settle for a plain, versatile sofa, try saving up for a distinctive chair. This one combines colour with modern curves.

LIVING ROOM TIP
If you want to make your own curtains but aren't much of a whiz with a sewing machine, cut out the stitching part of the process by using iron-on hemming and heading tape, available from haberdashery stores. You can also buy no-sew curtain kits which include full instructions

The look: A love of American 1930s style with touches of modernism and Art Deco glamour thrown in are the forces at work in this small living room. Fuss-free furnishings, natural colours and strong shapes add up to a sophisticated look.

Colour: The 1930s shade of chalky putty green on the walls gives a relaxing retro feel. The floorboards and woodwork are painted in off-white eggshell, a more congenial companion for the soft green than pure dazzling white. The plain whites and natural wood tones of furnishings and furniture are smartened up with accents of black, red and silver.

Furniture: A cow-print cushion brings Midwest style to the sofa, while the studded leather drawers of the storage unit and its row of cacti also bear the stamp of prairie chic. The Art Deco curve of the coffee table and the sculptural forms of the silver letters add impact. Open display shelving creates a freer feel than a built-in cupboard.

Fireplace: The fireplace, once concealed by a gas fire, has been opened up as a plain hole in the wall, with the surrounding plaster made good. An equally simple hearth has been created by sawing a space out of the floorboards and filling it with cement. A steel and mesh fireguard provides a sleek finishing touch.

Window: White muslin café curtains comprise the most minimal of dressings. Covering just the bottom half of the sash windows, they provide all the privacy that's needed while allowing light to flood in through the top.

LIVING ROOM TIP
A fireplace is a desirable feature in a living room and may help to sell your home when you want to move on, so don't block up the opening. Even a simple plastered-over hole can be a focal point. If you don't want a fire, use it as a display area for flowers or candles

The look: Many natural schemes are based on woody browns, so why not be different and put together a look inspired by pebbles or rocks? Stony greys give you the starting point for a sophisticated contemporary scheme.

Colour: Greys look cool and modern, but blending them with warmer neutrals such as fawn and beige prevents them from feeling too steely. Keep the overall look light – these walls are painted in a very pale grey, complemented by a beige carpet and an oatmeal-coloured sofa. You can then add darker shades of grey in throws, cushions and smaller pieces of furniture. Include a few more light browns for variety, plus accents of black for tonal variation.

Texture: Textured furnishings bring out the natural character of the scheme. The woven bouclé sofa upholstery mimics the roughness of stone, while the bobbles on the cushions look like tiny pebbles. Take the rough with the smooth, including soft suede alongside coarse but cosy wool and mohair. The curtains are in a lighter linen, fittingly patterned with a simple pebble motif.

Furniture: Neutral schemes have a strongly contemporary feel, so modern furniture suits this room. The curves of the oval table and the gently rounded shape of the sofa soften the look by varying the straight lines. The tall CD cabinet leads the eye upwards to add height.

Accessories: Abstract prints are a useful decorating tool if you want to add colour to pale walls: this one teams a large block of grey with a warmer pinkish brown. Vases with stony textures and rounded pebble-like shapes make perfect finishing touches.

The look: From pale grey to deepest indigo blues, sophisticated smoky shades are the epitome of cool. Mix rough textures with smooth in soft furnishings, combining wool, velvet and silk.

Colour: There is a wider range of greys than you might think, and using several together will save your scheme from seeming flat. The foreground wall is painted in a pale shade of ash, which tones with the carpet to provide barely-there colour that's a softer take on white. The back wall features a lilac-toned grey, which looks quite different. Having established contemporary cool with pale background colours, choose deeper, cosier shades to strike a more indulgent note with your soft furnishings, including one or two dark accents of indigo to add depth to the scheme.

Furniture: If you have the space for it, a large high-backed sofa gives a real feeling of luxury to a room. A big upholstered footstool will reinforce this and also double as extra seating, if only for pets! Keep remaining furniture simple and modern – steel and chrome are perfect partners for a grey scheme.

Soft furnishings: Sensual and shimmering fabrics lift greys from dull to decadent. Suede-effect upholstery looks and feels luxurious, while silvery cushions in pewter-coloured silk and velvet have a glamorous sheen. Include throws and cushions in warmer wools, both to vary the texture and boost comfort levels.

Accessories: A paper light shade, square lacquered dish and coloured glass vases and bowls with simple shapes give a nod to Japanese style. A circular pile rug punctuates the pale expanse of carpet with colour, texture and shape.

The look: Designers of modern homes put space at the top of their list. Big, bright and airy is what today's homebuyers want, and this showpiece room has it all – lofty proportions, expansive floor area and a battalion of the latest lighting technology and techniques.

Colour: The colour scheme is based on key contemporary favourites – white to increase the illusion of space, sleek wooden flooring for a clean but natural look and sophisticated lilac to make a feature of one wall. Against this minimalist backdrop, a palette of fashionable hues puts the focus on comfort areas – yellow and tan seating, deep purple curtains and rug, and a colourful line-up of lilac and lime cushions.

Feature wall: Every living room needs a focal point, and this one gives a cutting-edge twist to the conventional chimney breast and fireplace. A grate-like recess cut into the wall becomes an illuminated display area for pebbles and a pot plant. Three mirrors above draw the eye upwards to emphasize the room's roof-high headroom.

Furniture: The way furniture is arranged can make the difference between a welcoming and a barn-like atmosphere. A circular or U-shaped formation of sofas and chairs gives a sociable feel. The curvy turquoise coffee table and purple rug create an eye-catching centrepiece of design and colour.

Lighting: A number of different light sources are essential in a large space. A row of neat halogen spots beams out floor-level light from the base of the purple wall, while a trendy track system higher up carries lamps that can be adjusted to shine wherever needed.

LIVING ROOM TIP
Planning the layout of a living room is as important as deciding on a colour scheme. To make it easy, draw a floor plan to scale on squared paper and cut out separate shapes for pieces of furniture. Place these on the plan and move them around until you have an arrangement that suits your needs

The look: No space? No problem! Choose a colour scheme that makes your room appear to expand, add some invisible furniture and create a space-saving fireplace as a focal point. Tune in to the magic of minimalism and you can streamline the tiniest space.

Colour: The first step towards conquering that cramped feeling is to paint your walls white. This is the most effective shade for making interiors seem brighter, airier – and bigger. Team it with white flooring, and the dimensions of your room will realise their full potential. You can then use colours of your choice for furniture and soft furnishings – navy and grey warmed with accents of plum give a smart contemporary look.

Fireplace: A fireplace provides a great focal point, but the paraphernalia of hearth and surround may seem fussy and overwhelming in a tiny space. Keep things simple and create a minimalist hole-in-the-wall design that leaves the contours of the room clean and uncluttered. To convert your existing chimney breast, either follow the instructions provided by the manufacturer of the fire you buy or simply plaster over the inside of the hole and use it as a display space.

Furniture: It doesn't follow that you need a small sofa for a small room. One or two large items of furniture can give a less cluttered look than a number of smaller pieces. A sizeable sofa will add an impression of comfort to offset the chilliness of the white decor – emphasise this effect by choosing coloured upholstery and adding cushions and throws in soft or luxurious fabrics. Transparent furniture made from Perspex, acrylic or glass is a marvellous space booster as it appears almost invisible.

The look: Wooden flooring and streamlined furniture set the seal on a contemporary look, but this is no starkly minimalist scheme. Deep yellow gives a Mediterranean glow, while natural materials such as wicker create the comfort factor a family living room needs.

Colour: Sunny yellow will fill your room with positive energy and warmth, and also blends well with the natural tones of wood and wicker. To keep the look light and bright, team the strong colour with a pale wood flooring such as these limed oak planks. White freshens up the look and makes a feature of the simple brick fireplace, while a striped rug in neutral shades perks up the plain scheme with just a hint of pattern.

Furniture: Shape equals style, and furniture with flowing contemporary curves adds an extra element of interest to the overall look. A slatted wooden screen is functional as well as decorative; in a family room it acts as a clutter buster by hiding away children's toys.

Lighting: The wicker 'bottles' are large feature lamps – the bulb inside shines through the cane to cast fascinating patterns on surrounding objects, providing atmospheric lighting.

Window: Full-length muslin panels in contrasting colours make a dramatic treatment for the French windows, without blocking out too much light. If you can't find muslin the colour you want, try dyeing white lengths using cold water dyes, which are available in a wide range of shades from haberdashery stores.

LIVING ROOM TIP
Flexible lighting is essential for a living room. Aim to include three types of light source: ambient, for general illumination; task lamps, to focus on activities such as reading or sewing; and decorative lighting, which gives you the chance to introduce unusual and attractive fittings or interesting effects

The look: Modern colour power meets American Midwest style in this simple but striking scheme. Paintbox brights in strong shapes team with rustic wood and cow-print fabric for a warm, welcoming look that's full of fun.

Colour: If you've a yearning for dramatic colour, pick a mix of hues in shades as bright as they come and set them off against plain cream walls. Limit your choice to two or three colours – here orange and blue form an intense contrast, while a pink cushion adds a hot accent. The brown cushion reflects the deeper tones of the wooden furniture which, along with the laminate beech-block flooring, brings a pleasing natural warmth to the scheme.

Furniture: The rough wood and simple design of the coffee table give a rustic, backwoods feel, while a comfortably old-fashioned drawer unit provides storage for smaller items. Keeping furniture to a minimum increases the impact of the colourful seating. In this family room, large blue floorcushions provide inexpensive extra lounging space for a tribe of kids.

Blind: If you have an ugly window to conceal or an eyesore of a view beyond it, a blind with attitude is the answer. If you plan to keep it pulled down a lot, pick a fabric that makes a strong style statement such as this quirky cowhide print.

Accessories: A large potted cactus provides sculptural shape as well as reinforcing the Midwest theme, while abstract paintings in simple clip frames echo the bold colours of the furnishings. The planks of worn wood framing the mirror enhance the rustic feel.

The look: Neutral shades and natural textures bring out the best in each other to make livable decorating schemes. But natural needn't mean rustic – try a tender touch with soft fabrics in mellow tones to create a haven of contemporary comfort.

Colour: For a light but inviting atmosphere, choose a palette of warm mid-browns, such as tan, caramel and taupe, then add understated grey and vanilla to cut the richness without cooling the scheme. Painting walls in two different colours is an original way of adding interest to an all-neutral room. Make sure the two colours are of similar tones so that they balance each other.

Soft furnishings: Dress your sofa with throws and cushions in colours that melt into one another and fabrics that exude warmth. Top of the shopping list is anything that feels soft to the touch – tactile suede-effect fabric for a sofa cover or cube seating, a throw in plushy chenille and plenty of cushions in wool, mohair or fleecy finishes. Look for visually exciting textures too, such as knits or large-looped bouclé.

Furniture: Contemporary furniture balances the soft colours and surfaces with strong shapes. The eye-catching display boxes on the wall make excellent showcases for individual accessories and give a thoroughly modern look. It's easy to make your own from MDF, which can then be painted in gloss or eggshell for a more professional finish.

Floor: A carpet will help to boost the comfort factor. The ridged surface of this wool floorcovering gives it an extra dimension which adds to the textural mix in the room.

The look: Brilliant blocks of colour reminiscent of American West Coast style burst upon the wide open spaces of this large sun-filled room in a converted chocolate warehouse.

Conversion: Making a home in a converted warehouse is a tempting prospect, holding out the promise of open-plan loft-style living in rooms with acres of space. On the other hand, very large spaces can lack an intimate feel and are difficult to heat – this one has an underfloor system. You will also need vast quantities of paint and flooring to cover those expansive surfaces.

Colour: A large room can take dramatic colour contrasts that might seem overwhelming in a smaller space. Blue and orange are complementary colours – they lie directly opposite each other on the colour wheel – so they make a particularly compatible combination.

Painting the fireplace wall with a semicircle of orange is a creative way of adding both colour and shape to the large expanse of white. A yellow-centred rug radiates warmth at floor level. Patterned curtains bring together the three strong shades, which are otherwise used in bold blocks for maximum impact.

Furniture: Modern shapes work wonderfully in large rooms. The generously sized sofas have distinctive curvaceous lines which, along with the orange semicircle and the irregularly shaped coffee table, add form and focus to the room.

Glass wall: The art of division makes an open-plan space more livable. Glass bricks make an attractive and unobtrusive partition as they don't block the flow of light within the room. Here they are used to screen the front door and entrance area.

LIVING ROOM TIP
A colour wheel helps you avoid nasty clashes by taking the guesswork out of colour scheming. Learn how to use one (it's easy!) and you'll be able to see at a glance which shades are likely to work well together. Look for them in decorating books or interior design stores

The look: Streamlined storage and display units and dramatic blocks of colour against a seamless cream backdrop create a clean, minimalist look in a small room.

Colour: The shade of cream used on both the walls and floorboards is soft but space-enhancing, making the most of the light that flows unhindered through the undressed windows. Vivid shades of red and blue impact upon this bright backdrop, evoking the vibrant contrasts of a white-walled Mediterranean village. Used in bold blocks, they highlight the geometric shapes of the room as well as the designer-style storage unit and neat modern fireplace.

Storage and display:
The purpose-made MDF units combine space-saving storage with up-to-the-minute style. The blue unit forms an L-shape around a small sofa, and incorporates shelf and cupboard space as well as a display area on top. As a distinctive centrepiece, it makes a virtue of storage, avoiding the need to clutter the alcove with banks of shelves – all that's required there is space for TV equipment and CDs. Bringing the chimney breast forward by 15cm may seem a strange way of saving space but it allows for streamlined display, with a series of top-lit niches cut into the false wall.

Fireplace: A dummy fireplace cut into the same wall is lined with red mosaic tiles. Logs conceal a lava lamp which emits a flickering glow to create the illusion of flames.

Floor: Laying tongue-and-groove pine floorboards diagonally makes the room appear bigger. For sound insulation they are fixed to the existing boards using heavy-duty adhesive. Diluted cream emulsion gives them a sun-bleached look.

LIVING ROOM TIP
Lend extra emphasis to favourite accessories or pictures by giving them their own special lighting. Spotlights fitted into the top of display boxes or niches, or wall lamps that shine directly down onto prints or paintings, will increase their decorative value and impact

The look: A chiefly white colour scheme creates a fresh, contemporary look that boosts light and space. Make it feel comfortable rather than chilly with a relaxing blend of soft neutrals and natural materials.

Colour: Wall-to-wall white guarantees a light atmosphere. To make it livable, paint walls and flooring in a more forgiving off-white. Large expanses of any white can look cold, so the right wall is painted with subtle horizontal stripes in graduated shades of taupe, caramel and cream. A textured rug adds colour to the white-painted floor. Soften the look further with furnishings and fabrics in a selection of calming neutrals, keeping to the paler side of the spectrum to retain the airy, relaxed feel.

Natural materials: Wicker furniture and fibres such as cotton and linen are, literally, natural choices for neutral schemes. They add a relaxed feel as well as textural interest. The curtains are budget calico, the Roman blind is in linen and the sofa is upholstered in cotton twill.

Radiator cover: Radiators don't often rank high in the style stakes, but covers can disguise them. Wooden covers have fretwork grilles, to let heat through. Buy them in kit form, made to your measurements, then paint them to match your colour scheme.

Floor: A washed effect gives the floorboards just enough colour to conceal their yellowy tint. Sand and prepare your floor, then brush on a mixture of two parts matt emulsion to three parts water. Add a few more coats until you get the desired effect, allowing each to dry. Finish with water-based, clear-drying matt varnish.

CONTEMPORARY

The look: Dramatic colour schemes may fall short of their intended impact if the eye is distracted by piles of clutter. Make sure your schemes include stylish storage solutions to cater for all the ephemera of in-home entertainment.

Colour: Bright blue forms a dynamic contrast with the sharp yellow on the walls and the warm wood tones of the furniture. The white carpet brings light relief, and its ridged bouclé finish adds a touch of texture to the scheme. The restrained two-colour designs on the cushions and the bolder swirls of the rug introduce pattern and pace, breaking up the plain blocks of blue.

Furniture: Furniture on wheels is both stylish and flexible as it's easy to shift around. Castors are especially useful on large, heavy units –

a shelving system on wheels does double duty as a room divider but can be moved in seconds when you want to open up the space. A coffee table that incorporates storage is handy for stashing magazines, while a glass top helps to maintain a spacious look. The beech stool also offers storage space beneath its removable top. The sofa is covered in fake suede and the patterned cushions are made from linen union.

Wall storage: Wall-mounted storage keeps surfaces clear of clutter. CD collections can soon get out of hand, but purpose-designed racks display them attractively. For books and accessories, wall shelves are a popular storage solution – look for adjustable systems so that you can vary the distance between the shelves to accommodate items of different sizes.

LIVING ROOM TIP
Storage on open shelves becomes display, so consider what you want to show off. Shelves crammed with books look fine if you like a library effect, but interspersing them with ornaments or pictures gives a lighter, more attractive look

The look: Woody browns and plant greens create a warm, earthy feel. Keep the look rich with natural materials, from wood and bamboo to linen and cotton, and let texture play its part with nubbly fabrics and open weaves.

Colour: Brown may seem dull if used as a flat paint colour, but this wall has a subtly graduated finish, with three different shades blending seamlessly from darkest on the left to lightest on the right. Wooden furniture and accessories contribute their own natural colours, which are reflected in the neutral tones of the sofa and cushion fabrics. To keep the look interesting, include a variety of different neutrals, from dark brown to pale beige, and add accents of pistachio and jungle greens.

Wall: To give your wall a graduated effect, measure and divide it into three equal vertical bands. Paint each with a different shade, starting with the darkest on the left. Then, where they meet, blend them together with a brush before the paint dries. For the best effect, hire a compressor spray gun from a specialist paint or hire shop. Spray on each colour, overlapping slightly with the last to blend.

Texture: Supplement natural colours with rough-textured flooring and fabrics for that down-to-earth feel. The bouclé-upholstered sofa is covered with cushions in hessian, linen and slubby silks, while the carpet is textured paper. Different forms of wood grain, from mahogany-style laminate to natural bamboo, also enrich the look.

Accessories: Complement the leafy jungle theme with oriental-style lamps and accessories. Look for vases made from bamboo, and others with simple shapes in browns and greens.

The look: If you want a living room you can really snuggle up in, decorate with a spectrum of deliciously warm, glowing colours. Add big sofas with sumptuous upholstery which are just made to sink into.

Colour: The yellow on the walls reflects and brightens the natural light that flows in through the large window. Choose a buttery shade like this and you'll avoid the green glow that some yellows take on under artificial light. Balance it with lively orange and deep plum – using each as a sizeable area of plain colour gives the scheme its striking sense of simplicity and richness. Honey-toned wood in flooring and furniture blends beautifully with the glowing hues for all-round warmth.

Furniture: With high sides and soft velvety upholstery to match their hot colours, the sofas look invitingly cosy.

A footstool adds a further touch of comfort. Old wooden chests provide casual table and display space while doubling as capacious storage containers. Found in a junk shop, these have been carefully stripped and waxed to enhance the beauty of the wood.

Window: Venetian blinds create a fuss-free contemporary window treatment. Venetians with wooden slats have a more natural, laid-back look than metallic ones, and tone comfortably with wooden furniture and warm colours.

Accessories: A hint of glamour comes from the touches of gold and silver which are introduced in the shiny metallic bowl on the coffee table, the golden centre of the clock face and the gilt frames of the pictures. The rough-textured cream vase and wooden lampbase add a more rustic note.

The look: This futuristic scheme makes full use of flowing modern shapes and vivid colour contrasts to create a bold and unconventional look. The stunning chaise longue and the warm, passionate quality of the pinks add a sense of glamorous decadence and comfort.

Colour: Using two bright and strongly contrasting colours in a big way is sure to create a dramatic effect. For maximum impact, blue and pink paint shades feature in equal amounts, on neighbouring walls, with the curtain colours continuing the pink across the window. Concentric painted circles in both shades help to heighten the contrast between the colours while breaking up the expanse of plain wall. Carrying a strong colour theme through to furniture and accessories will embolden it further, and ensures that shapely pieces grab their fair share of the attention.

Furniture: Shape can make as strong a statement as colour, and the flowing modern curves of the chaise longue and chair break the mould of furniture design. Perfect for a trendy setting, they are joined by a contemporary wheeled storage unit with slick chrome frame and blue drawers.

Window: The vivid pinks of the roller blind and gathered curtains frame the window to ensure that it plays its full part in the colour drama. However, the sheer curtains allow natural light to shine through, preventing their strong shade from making the room feel too dark.

Accessories: Coloured glass accessories add reflective highlights which help to brighten the effect of the deep colours. The cactus adds further striking shape to the room, while the pink maribou trim on the blue cushion enhances the glamorous feel.

The look: This is where town meets country, in a classy look that combines elegant furniture with warm red walls, and chic stripes with feminine florals.

Colour: Raspberry red and cream make a delicious mix. Use the red on the walls and your room will instantly take on a warmer feel. To keep the look contemporary, team it with a light carpet, curtains and sofa cover, then add further elements of pink and dark red in smaller furnishings such as cushion or table covers.

Pattern: Elements of pattern help to add pace and impact to a scheme, and to define its character. The stripes on the cushions and table cover add a classic touch, while a single floral print – the loose chair cover – softens the scheme and evokes a comforting country feel. For a unified look, keep your key colours running through all the patterns in the room.

Furniture: A plain white sofa forms a stark contrast with rich red walls, but add a pile of coloured cushions in soft, sensual fabrics such as velvet and wool, and it immediately takes on a cosier air. Your coffee table may already suit the look, but fitting it with a cover of deep red fabric can help to strengthen the colour scheme. The traditional-style armchair and wrought-iron side table add townhouse elegance to this room, while the white wood and wicker chair has country appeal.

Window: The cream curtains, made from a cotton and linen mix, have bands of red striped fabric stitched on to give them a stronger look alongside the dark walls.

The look: Spring greens freshen the atmosphere in this room to balance the somewhat gloomy effect of the black-grated Victorian fireplace. Natural tones and textures relax the look further.

Colour: The walls are painted in a soft minty green, creating an environment that's both refreshing and tranquil. Bands of sharper apple shades around the top make the room seem wider without detracting from its height. The natural quality of the greens is complemented by the wooden floorboards and chest, and by the rustic colour and texture of the hessian sofa cover. Cushions give this a lift with further subtle greens in restrained checks and florals.

Fireplace: With its black grate and surround of orange pine, the fireplace was overpowering the small room, so the pine has been given a limed effect using diluted cream-coloured emulsion, which calms it and makes it blend with the walls. The floral hearth tiles echo the hydrangea print used for one cushion.

Furniture: The cheapest way of making existing furniture fit a new scheme is to add loose covers. While the sofa has a full outfit of hessian, a simple calico cover turns an old wooden chest into a slick coffee table. The blue chair tones with hints of blue in the hydrangea print, so didn't need a cover.

Storage: The lidded chest doubles as a surface for the hi-fi and storage for items that aren't needed every day. Small, inexpensive MDF drawer units are just the right size for CDs, and can be wall-mounted. A box shelf provides display space for accessories.

The look: Softer than purple and more sophisticated than red, plum oozes comfort and style. For a luxuriously decadent living room, warm up a chilly cream scheme with layers of succulent shades, from the deepest black tones of a ripe Victoria plum to juicy damson reds.

Colour: For a plum scheme that's alluring but not overpowering, keep your background light. The off-white carpet and woodwork enhance the richness of the cream walls, which make a perfect foil for the warm shades of the soft furnishings. Blend plains, plaids and stripes in different tones of plum – the patterns help to break up the intensity of solid colour. Add glassware and candles in dark plum tones to continue the colour onto sideboards and mantel.

Furniture: A sofa covered in a strokable plushy fabric and heaped with cushions reinforces the decadence of the scheme. Furniture in a mix of styles matches the elegance of the past with the simplicity of the present. A modern footstool doubles as a coffee table, while the armchair and chest of drawers introduce a comforting touch of tradition that adds to the luxury of the look.

Fireplace: Leaving a fireplace without a surround gives a plain, modern look, although the open brickwork and wooden mantelshelf strike a rustic note. Their dark colours tone with the plum shades.

Carpet: A pale carpet won't stay that way for long if it has to withstand the patter of tiny feet, but for a grown-up scheme it's a luxury worth having. For comfort and durability, choose a short-pile design in wool, which is naturally hard-wearing.

LIVING ROOM TIP
Pure wool carpets are luxuriously soft underfoot, but for rooms that receive heavy traffic a mix of 80 per cent wool to 20 per cent nylon is a more hard-wearing choice

The look: If florals conjure up images of some great aunt's curtains, take a look at the latest fabric designs. Let your room blossom with sparsely patterned flower prints and ethereal leaf motifs in one or two colours. These patterns sit comfortably with today's pared-down interiors to introduce a new take on old world charm.

Colour: Put the spotlight on the fabrics by keeping the backdrop plain and understated, choosing similar pale neutrals for your walls, sofa and carpet. Cream gives a more relaxing look than white and also makes a softer partner for the muted colours of the cushions and throw. For an elegant look, choose mainly dusky pinks and powdery blues rather than girly candy colours.

Pattern: For a fresh approach to florals, remember less is more. Intermittent sprays of flowers on a plain throw, loosely painted roses scattered sparingly across a cream curtain and small panels of exquisite embroidery on cushions take the place of busy, all-over prints. Mix patterns in varying sizes, from one large-scale design through smaller motifs to tiny spriggy prints. Subtle self-patterned furnishings such as the sofa cover and blue cushion are ideal for this look.

Fabrics: Texture can be as important as pattern in creating mood. Crisp cottons work best at the window for a fresh, contemporary feel, but cushions and throws can become a focus for luxury, with delicate silks and satins, beaded detailing and ribbon trim.

Accessories: Continue the theme with carefully chosen accessories – a lampshade with an abstract flower motif, a print showing a single bud and, of course, a few real flowers informally arranged.

LIVING ROOM TIP
Jazz up plain curtains or cushion covers with trimmings to make them match the mood of your room. Snap up odd remnants as and when you find them and start a collection you can dip into when you fancy

The look: Breathe fresh air into country style with walls the colour of a summer sky. This relaxed scheme relies on just a few traditional features to make a subtle statement – an upholstered chair in checked fabric, one or two cushions and an old-fashioned radiator – but the overall look is light and modern.

Colour: Paint the walls in a refreshing blue that blows away the cobwebs and replaces them with an upbeat contemporary feel. Plain painted surfaces keep the look clean – decorate woodwork in white for a crisp contrast. Wooden floorboards suit both country and modern interiors – finish them with a mid-tone stain and matt varnish for a wholesome look.

Furniture: Pattern has its part to play in a country scheme, but less is more. Forget flower-spattered chintz, and cover chairs and sofas in smart checks or textured plains, adding just a few floral cushions. Give way to the comfort factor when choosing seating – it's nice to sink into a roomy armchair – but keep occasional furniture simple. The wicker footstool combines natural texture with slick design, while a garden-style metal table adds a casual touch.

Window: Pared-down window treatments bring the country look up to date – conventional curtains give way to gauzy panels and crisp blinds. This window has a double-layered café-style blind in gingham and voile, to provide varying degrees of privacy, which is supplemented by white-painted wooden shutters that can be closed when required.

The look: An abundance of rustic pine in flooring, furniture and fittings is complemented by a rich but relaxing shade of russet to give this room its cosy log-cabin feel.

Colour: A warm and earthy wall colour will enhance the beauty of wooden furniture and flooring – choose a muted shade that blends with its natural grain. To prevent the strong colour from seeming overpowering, add a fresh contrast with white sofa and chair covers. The rug, cushions and pictures introduce additional colour accents, ranging from rich reds, golds and pinks to darker blues and browns. Plants complement the wall colour with their dark green foliage, while enhancing the country feel.

Furniture: Chunky wooden furniture suits this look – search out solidly built chests and trunks with plain, serviceable designs. Make the most of the wood by using waxes rather than polishes to get it gleaming.

Door: To maximize the rustic feel, choose wooden fittings as well as furniture. If you aren't lucky enough to have wooden doors, salvage or reclamation yards are a good source of traditional panelled designs. This door has been rehung so that it opens against the wall, making more efficient use of space in the room.

Windows: Like the skirtings, the window frames have had their painted finish stripped away to provide the room with yet more natural wood. The narrow windows are dressed with tea-coloured Roman blinds that tone with the russet walls.

LIVING ROOM TIP
Paint radiators to match the walls, to make them blend in. If you can't find a special radiator paint in your colour, a coat of multi-surface primer followed by oil-based gloss or eggshell will do the trick. Make sure the radiator is cold before you start

The look: This scheme gathers together a mix of tactile natural textures to create a relaxed rustic feel within a modern setting. Soothing soft-toned blues help give the cool stoney hues a lift.

Colour and texture: To paint your walls, choose a muted mid-tone blue that's strong enough to balance the earthy neutrals, yet not so bright or intense that it overpowers them. The curtains frame the window with a darker denim shade, leaving the natural tones and textures to dominate the lower part of the room. Nubbly fabrics and carpeting in a warm blend of camels, taupes and browns re-create the rugged appearance of old stone, while wooden furniture and natural accessories also add to the visual feast.

Furniture: Look for furniture that combines modern shapes with appropriate textures or finishes, such as the bouclé-covered sofa and limed chest of drawers. Or try using paint effects to create the look of worn wood – the coffee table has been painted with a light woodwash.

Carpet: Carpets with chunky looped or woven textures are trendy, practical and ideal for this look. They are available in natural fibres such as seagrass and coir, which are extremely hard-wearing, and also in wool, which is warmer underfoot and easier to keep clean. Mid-tones are more practical than very light or dark colours as both tend to show any marks.

Accessories: This room keeps the rustic versus modern theme going with a seagrass basket, grass cushion and twiggy lampshade near floor level and slick contemporary accessories higher up.

The look: To transplant country comfort into a tiny townhouse, steer clear of fussy patterns and settle for a plainer style. This more sophisticated version of the rustic look requires just one or two natural elements – a pile of logs or the odd piece of pine furniture – to give a country twist to a light, contemporary backdrop.

Colour: In a small room, boost the illusion of space with walls in white or pale cream, continuing this shade over features such as the fire surround and shelves. Then develop the rustic theme with earthy tones and natural materials. The terracotta hearth tiles and honey-coloured coffee table help to warm up the scheme, while the brown throw adds colour to the white sofa. Gold and red accents in the tea glasses and striped cushion introduce a touch of glamour.

Furniture: Not only does a white sofa keep the overall look light, it's also a good investment as it goes with virtually any colour scheme. It can always be brightened up with throws and cushions. Relax into the rustic look with smaller pieces of wooden furniture – the coffee table is an old pine chest.

Shelving: Alcoves lend themselves well to storage or display – with shelves fitted all the way across, they make natural bookcases. No space is wasted – the area underneath the lower shelf serves as a log store right beside the fire.

Mirror: A large mirror forms a decorative feature above a fireplace but also serves a more practical purpose in a tiny room by reflecting plenty of light and adding to the sense of space.

The look: Mellow yellows complement natural wood for a look that's as warm and sunny as a summer cornfield. Fresh checks in poppy reds and cornflower blues give the rustic tones a modern edge.

Colour: Yellow is guaranteed to lift the spirits. It also blends beautifully with glowing wood tones, so is a particularly charismatic colour if country cheer is what you're after. Two shades are used on these walls, one pale and one bright. Instead of relaxing into floral elegance, the scheme goes for bold modern colour contrasts with lively checks in red and blue, using them as impact-adding accents in the window blind, table runner and cushions covers.

Wall panelling: The walls are covered to about two-thirds of the way up with wood panelling, which evokes a country-house feel. Tongue-and-groove planks are widely available from DIY stores and timber merchants, and anyone with reasonable DIY skill can cut them to size and fix them in place. They can then be painted – if you combine two different shades on your walls, always use the darker one on the lower part.

Furniture: Wooden furniture is a vital part of the look, but avoid anything too dark or heavy. Look for unfussy contemporary pieces with mellow or blond tones and supplement them with further natural texture in the form of shapely wicker and modern woven chairs.

Accessories: The tall bulrushes, the leaf and twig pictures on the walls and the jute fringing that trims the plain cushions strengthen the room's wholesome country charm, while cream-coloured ceramic and wooden vases with simple organic shapes reinforce its modern edge.

LIVING ROOM TIP
Tongue-and-groove boards and wood panelling not only give a room character but can also conceal uneven or cracked walls which would require lengthy preparation if they were to be painted or papered

The look: More often seen in a traditional gentleman's study or a slick bachelor pad, a rugged leather sofa can look equally at home among pretty pastels and floral fabrics. Bring out its feminine side with a lilac and white scheme reminiscent of cool New England style.

Colour: The delicate lilac wall colour and the fresh white woodwork and furnishings create a modern airy effect, while the glowing wood floor reflects the natural warmth of the sofa. The sombre brown leather is given a lift by the boldly flowered cushions, which include mauves and pinks that tone with both the walls and sofa.

Furniture: White wooden furniture creates a clean modern-country feel. The classic design of the console table strikes a note of small-town elegance, while the sturdy chest used as a coffee table injects a more casual air. Both pieces have pine tops that echo the wooden flooring. The armchair is traditional in style, while the leather sofa has straighter, modern lines.

Window: A voile blind with the same design as the cushions dresses the window, adding a light wall of flowers behind the sofa to provide further contrast with the dark leather. The blind is supplemented by white-painted wooden shutters.

Accessories: To add comfort to the cool scheme, a fluffy flokati rug punctuates the wooden floor, and a pale pink cashmere throw is draped over the leather sofa. On the mantelpiece, pretty tea glasses and a striped jug add pink accents that echo the colours of the floral cushions. Simple flower prints introduce further floral touches.

LIVING ROOM TIP
Make sure rugs have a non-slip backing to prevent accidents when used on polished wooden floors. Paint the back of cheap rugs with PVA adhesive, which dries to form a rubbery coating. For others you can buy anti-slip underlay, which comes in a range of sizes

The look: The huge brickwork fireplace dominates this room, inviting intimate family gatherings around its glowing embers. Old wooden chests enhance the homely feel, but striking colour contrasts enliven the look.

Colour: The dazzling primrose yellow used on the walls turns on the sunshine to fill the room with cheerful colour. The cream-coloured carpet and rug also help to offset the dark tones of the brickwork and wooden furniture, while providing a soft and comfortable floorcovering that adds to the room's warm, cosy atmosphere. As red and green are complementary colours, the two sofas create a dramatic contrast that increases the energizing impact of the colour scheme.

Fireplace: The fireplace has all the rustic natural texture that country style demands. The surround and chimney breast are built from reclaimed bricks and incorporate a mantelshelf in rough unfinished wood. The hearth tiles are made of stone.

Furniture: Solid wooden trunks and chests not only have oodles of character but also serve a dual purpose, as storage containers and tables. A round wooden table makes a shapely display area for another traditional-style feature – a collection of framed family photos. The sofas and trunks are arranged in symmetrical style, flanking the fireplace to stress its role as the focal point.

Window: With such vigorous colour contrasts, the room needs little pattern, but the woven leaf design of the cream-coloured curtains adds textural interest. Choose a curtain pole that matches your scheme – this chunky wooden design with rounded finials is made for a country look.

The look: Choose an energizing yellow to give your room that feelgood factor, then mellow the mood with mauve. Painted wood, boldly checked curtains and scalloped furniture add cheery country charm to the colourful scheme.

Colour: Complementary colours – two lying directly opposite each other on the colour wheel – bring out the best in one another. Cool mauve contrasts strongly with zingy yellow but calms it down at the same time, creating a scheme that's strikingly colourful but also easy to live with. This room includes a range of mauves, from the pale lavender carpet to the lilac-painted table to the deep purple accents in the curtains, which also feature yellow to unite the two key colours.

Furniture: The sofa covers are in a deep, bluish mauve which is bold enough to balance the yellow walls. Cushions give them a lift with lighter shades of lilac and pink, plus a floral patchwork print. The wooden furniture has been painted to fit the scheme. The top of the coffee table has a grained effect, achieved by using a special tool to comb through the paint while still wet, creating a woodgrain pattern. The scalloped trim has been cut from strips of MDF and glued in place, but you can buy ready-made decorative edgings if you don't fancy cutting your own.

Window: The curtains have a contemporary tab-top heading and hang from a stainless steel pole. In a room where the walls and furniture are in contrasting colours, long curtains can be used to continue the second colour up to ceiling level, juxtaposing it more effectively with the walls.

LIVING ROOM TIP
Sew your curtains with deep lower hems to help them hang nicely. You can also add small metal weights inside the hem, which prevent lighter materials from blowing around when the window is open

The look: Floral prints don't necessarily mean chintz. Today's contemporary patterns work wonderfully in most settings, but forget the traditional associations if you want a contemporary look. Used here with crisp whites and fresh modern ginghams, they have an up-to-date edge.

Colour: White walls give a plain base to work with, while wooden floorboards balance their chilling effect with natural warmth. Choose a single colour to unify the floral prints – here they all include varying shades of pink or red.

Pattern: The key to mixing florals is to use just one large-scale print, and then add to it with smaller bud designs. Build your scheme with ginghams and narrow stripes. Try using up to three patterned fabrics on one bolster by making panels from different prints

in your scheme. But don't go overboard on the number of patterns in a room – make four your limit.

Furniture: A white sofa is a plain foil for the crowd of patterned cushions. The floral cover on the armchair introduces a larger area of pattern, its big blooms giving the room a change of pace in contrast with the tiny bud designs. Stick to scaled-down prints to cover smaller items of furniture such as the footstool. Comfortable traditional-style seating looks best with floral upholstery, but keep the look modern by adding simple white tables that blend in effortlessly with the background.

Windows: Fancy ruched blinds give a prettier look than straight Roman or roller designs. Adding a striped trim to a floral-print blind turns it into an instant eye-catcher.

LIVING ROOM TIP
A large sofa can be an expensive purchase, so choose a timeless design if you plan to invest in quality. Plain upholstery is more versatile than patterned, but remember you can always give your sofa a new look by having loose covers made

The look: Zingy lime green, a blend of cool blues and a clutch of punchy patterns put a contemporary spin on a room that also makes the most of its more traditional elements.

Colour: Blue and green often make perfect partners, even if the shades used are very different in tone. In this room, vivacious lime green walls are balanced by deep, dependable blues – a rich ultramarine for the curtains and a more muted cobalt for the carpet. The top of the walls and the ceiling are painted in white to add a feeling of space and height.

Pattern: Totally coordinated furnishings, where all the prints come from the same range of designs, can give too contrived a look, so follow this room's example and choose individual designs if you want to use a lot of pattern. The way to make them work together is to stick to a limited colour palette. Bold checks and large florals form an invigorating mix, but all feature blue or lime, or both.

Furniture: In a smallish room, two medium-sized sofas can make better use of space than the traditional three-piece suite, and also allow for a more balanced, symmetrical look. The pine coffee table, with its circular shape and rounded legs, provides a contrast of form with the straight lines of the fireplace.

Accessories: An elegant screen and fire irons add the finishing touches to the working fireplace. A few fresh lime green flowers and some foliage in a glass vase introduce a fresh touch that brings the colour scheme to life.

The look: This large living-cum-dining room is designed to resemble a light and airy beach house, hence the sky and sea colours, whitewashed boards and beachcomber works of art.

Colour: A vision of an idyllic beach scene always comes with a cloudless sky, which is what this deep blue paint seeks to convey. Beech-look laminate flooring and wall panelling with a weathered effect are reminiscent of whitewashed beach huts, while the large-checked rag rugs add sea shades of green and aqua. All that's needed to complete the picture are sand and sun, and the painted wooden furniture introduces enough cheery yellow to represent both.

Walls: The walls are panelled up to dado height with simple boarding, which is painted to give the weathered look. If your room does not already have a dado rail, buy lengths of moulding from a DIY store and fix them in place first, then nail panels of wall board below this. Paint both the dado and panelling white, then lightly sand them when dry to expose the wood.

Furniture: Painting the sideboard, dining table and coffee table in matching yellow gives the furniture a unified look. Casual rattan chairs lend the scheme seaside style, while the sofa and armchair have covers in colours that match the overall decor.

Accessories: Trendy fisherman's lampshades and a wicker picnic basket are in keeping with the theme, while a more immediate suggestion of the seashore comes from shells and pebbles. The beachcomber wall decorations are made from whitewashed timber joists, which have shells, pebbles and strips of driftwood glued on top.

The look: This scheme relies on texture rather than colour for impact, with a selection of natural furniture, fabrics and accessories all contributing to the subtle interplay of surfaces.

Colour and texture: Neutrals are the ultimate play-it-safe choice for walls and floors. Creams and beiges go with anything, ensure a spacious atmosphere and have a clean, contemporary appeal. Using neutrals throughout your room requires care though, as your blank canvas can soon become a boring one if it has no real colour. Bring earthy tones into focus by choosing furnishings with textural interest – herringbone-weave carpeting, woven furniture and wicker baskets – and including a variety of natural materials, from wood to leather. The contrasts between them will enrich the overall look, and a few colourful accessories will heighten the impact.

Furniture: The furniture includes a variety of textures and tones. The smoothness of the tan leather armchair and blond wood chest contrast with the ribbed sofa fabric and the woven banana-leaf stool, which serves as a coffee table.

Accessories: Texture is the key consideration when buying accessories – wicker and wood storage boxes and cushions with raffia fringing add further natural charm, while the dark carved wood of the mirror frame has a pretty floral pattern. The orange vase and pink and mauve cushions add tiny amounts of colour to perk up the scheme.

Window: Subtle looks need plenty of light to show off textural detail, so don't block it out with heavy curtains. Light sheers looped onto a wooden pole provide privacy, while at the same time allowing sunshine to filter through.

The look: Robust colour makes a bold statement, especially when there is little clutter to distract the eye. However, the owner's minimalist principles do allow a few comforts, such as the pretty cast-iron fireplace which adds heart to the scheme.

Colour: Strong turquoise covers the walls for maximum impact. A white cover shows off the shapely form of the armchair against the dark background, and makes a striking contrast with the black fireplace. Country-style checks in subtler shades on a chair and cushion soften the look.

Fireplace: The cast-iron fireplace is from a reclamation yard. These places are treasure troves of original fittings taken from older homes. If your period fireplace is beyond repair, see if you can find a genuine replacement before opting for a modern lookalike. You may need to do a little restoration – this one was covered in white paint, which was stripped by the yard owner. The metal is finished with black polish.

Furniture: Minimalism is a modern concept, but that doesn't mean it requires space-age furniture. Just make sure that the few pieces you include are either beautiful or useful, preferably both! Here, a couple of traditional chairs provide comfy seating, while an old African stool makes an unusual centrepiece. Clutter is hidden away in the cupboard.

Floor: Many older houses still have original floorboards which, when stripped and varnished, look great with modern country decor. If your boards are in good condition, strip them using drum and edging sanders borrowed from a local hire shop, who will show you how to use them. Seal the sanded surface with two coats of acrylic varnish.

The look: Clean up with dazzling white for a scheme that's as bright as can be. Although only a few hints of colour and texture disturb the snowy expanse, decorative furniture and accessories steer this scheme well away from stark minimalism.

Colour: Wall-to-wall white guarantees an air of space and light but may seem clinical or chilly, especially in a north-facing room. If you plump for a total whitewash, relax the look with touches of texture and colour. Here texture is provided by the rough wood of the table and chair and the craggy pebbles and smooth slate tiles of the fireplace. Blue accents appear in the patterned blinds and the checked upholstery of the wooden seat, while scatter cushions add splashes of lime, lemon and pink.

Floor: The floorboards are lightened with liming wax, which gives them a white finish to match the walls while allowing the natural wood grain to show through.

Furniture: Painting furniture white lends it a clean, contemporary look, whatever its style. The wooden sofa originated as a *howdah*, for riding on an elephant, and has been stripped, painted and upholstered. The Lloyd Loom chair is also painted – use spray paint on woven fibres or wicker to cover the weave fully.

Accessories: In a room with little colour, accessories add vital decoration. Look for eye-catching shapes such as the tall curly candleholder and modern wire chandelier, and punctuate expanses of white wall with pictures.

LIVING ROOM TIP
If you want to liven up a roomful of white or cream walls, try painting the woodwork in a colour. You could also use colour to highlight any period details such as picture and dado rails or cornices

The look: A scheme based on plain neutrals gets a colourful lift from a set of loose covers. Easy to make and even simpler to swap for others when it's time to change your look, these fabric disguises can be used to dress up chairs, tables or even sofas if you feel keen.

Colour: Neutrals go with any colour, so decorating the shell of your room in shades such as taupe or beige provides a versatile blank canvas. If you want to play it completely safe, stick to pale neutrals for larger items such as sofas and curtains as well as walls. You can then use loose covers and accessories to make a colour statement. Here aqua and lime freshen up the neutral scheme to give a spring-like feel. If you want a cosier look for autumn, just sew a new set of covers in warmer colours.

Loose covers: Fabric covers can be made to fit tables and chairs closely but are also easy to remove for washing. Measure your furniture carefully, then make a paper pattern. To save making mistakes on good fabric, do a test run using calico or sheeting. Once you've got the fit right, the test piece can be unpicked and the pieces used as a pattern.

Window: If you like flowing curtains but want a contemporary look, choose a tab-top heading. Here the tabs loop smartly over a slender metal pole, while the brushed denim curtains are longer than full-length so that they form luxurious pools of fabric on the floor. Cut your curtains twice as wide as the window, joining two or more lengths if necessary to get the required width.

LIVING ROOM TIP
Make sure that any fabrics you use for upholstery and curtains are flame retardant. All new sofas have to meet strict fire regulations but second-hand ones may have been made before they came into force

The look: Neutral shades can appear a little bland on their own, so throw in a handful of leafy greens to liven them up. Subtle patterns and natural textures also weave their magic to perk up plain looks.

Colour: To help prevent neutrals from seeming flat, include a range of tones. Walls in a very pale beige reflect the pinkish shades of the carpet to form a warm background for the woody browns of the furniture. The cream sofa appears richer in contrast with the bright white of the fireplace and woodwork. The greens that sharpen up the scheme appear as accent colours in the cushions, raffia bowls and lamp. The role of accents is to lend impact to a scheme by adding small amounts of an extra colour, often a contrast with the main shades.

Furniture: Textured furnishings are also useful for livening up a natural scheme. The weave of the chair, the herringbone stripe of the sofa, and the ribbed cushions and bobbly throw provide a medley of touchy-feely fabrics. Furniture in natural materials, such as wicker, rattan and wood, also brings texture.

Carpet: A scheme rich in texture doesn't need much pattern, but the odd subtle design can add extra interest. The carpet's two-tone pattern is easy on the eye: its colours blend harmoniously with the other shades in the room, and its design reflects the leafy theme.

Accessories: Both real and artificial leaves can be used as accessories. Arrow reeds and palm sprays create a jungle feel, while a leafy picture and tiles adorn the wall and mantelpiece alongside a fossil and other treasures from the natural world.

The look: Vibrant accent colours set against a backdrop of space-enhancing neutrals make this room look light but lively. Using pale creams and beiges that are soft in tone creates a soothing atmosphere.

Colour: Although the room has a higher-than-average ceiling and a generous bay window, it isn't huge, so choosing neutrals for the walls, flooring and curtains maintains the sense of space. For cosiness, the walls are painted in a creamy tone with some depth, and the woodwork and ceiling are in soft rather than brilliant white. The neutral carpet has texture, which introduces a hint of pattern without enclosing the space. A rug in earthy tones helps to ground the scheme and define the seating area. Accents of terracotta and hot pink add warmth and pace.

Furniture: Don't assume small furniture will create a greater feeling of space; pieces that look chunky and imposing add structure and form, even in a room with limited proportions. The large sofa and chair have upright arms which make the seats appear deep and comfortable, and using a big upholstered footstool as a coffee table enhances the cosy, comfy feel.

Window: A bold terracotta border gives the cream curtains added punch. Trimming pale curtains in this way also helps to protect the leading edge from fingermarks. They hang from a slender stainless steel pole bent to fit the bay.

Accessories: Bins, boxes and baskets are useful for adding bright accent colour, which should only be used in small amounts. Cushions and throws add softer shades, plus a mix of cosy textures. The abstract picture is big and bold to balance the furniture.

LIVING ROOM TIP
Choose a curtain pole that extends at least 15cm beyond the window recess on either side. This allows the curtains to be pulled well back for maximum light, and also makes the window appear wider

The look: Clear the air with a palette of powdery pastels. Delicate blues, lilacs and pinks turn down the colour tempo for a look that's beautifully feminine without being too sweet or sugary.

Colour: To set a sophisticated tone, use cool blues and lilacs for walls and curtains. You can then add warmth with accents of pink or pale orange in cushions and other accessories. These walls are painted in two shades of soft blue, with the lighter tone in a band above picture-rail level, which has the effect of making the high ceiling seem lower and the room feel cosier.

Furniture: The white furniture and fireplace keep the look light. Elegant lines suit the feminine mood, but this doesn't mean filling your room with expensive antiques. A shapely modern stool and a garden table with curvy metal frame create an informal, easy-living feel that's spot-on for contemporary chic.

Window: Light window treatments are a must for this look, and a double layer of translucent drapes works as well as one heavier curtain, providing volume without weight. Roman blinds in white linen provide privacy at the overlooked window, while a full-length curtain in fine cotton adds romantically flowing fabric and subtle pattern as well as an additional screen in the evening.

Accessories: The light touch continues with delicate glassware and a slim metal lamp. Cushions give you the opportunity to add further colour and pattern – but don't overdo the florals if you want to retain the sophisticated feel. A jug of fresh flowers can be more eloquent than a sofa heaped with chintzy blooms!

LIVING ROOM TIP
For a no-sew heading on light curtains, use pincer clips that simply grip the top of the fabric. They also let you turn tablecloths, throws and saris into instant curtains – fold over the top to adjust them to the right length and make a decorative valance

LAID-BACK

The look: Let your sweet side show with a palette of delicious berry colours – blueberry, raspberry and cherry pink. Then add cream, with white stained or painted furniture that sits perfectly against the berry backdrop.

Colour: For a fresh, summery feel, keep your cool with a background of blues, then add warmer pinks in smaller doses, as cushions and throws. Most walls here are painted in a pale icy blue, but the one behind the armchair is highlighted in a deeper blueberry, which strengthens the scheme without overwhelming the room. It is echoed by a rug in a similar shade which adds colour and bold geometric pattern to the white-painted floorboards. The view through the doorway reveals that the berry theme continues in the hallway, the glimpse of pink wall reinforcing the sweetening effect of the raspberry and cherry colours used in the living room.

Furniture: Mix old and new for that easy-living feel of summer. An oriental-style screen can easily make friends with an old-fashioned bench. White-painted wooden furniture with a distressed finish suits both the mood and colours of the scheme. Cream upholstery on sofas and armchairs looks fresh, and is perfect for showing off coloured cushions and throws.

Soft furnishings: Enrich the plain scheme with a mix of patterns and textures. Simple ticking stripes and two-tone floral or paisley designs give a light, pretty look. Textured throws in warm fabrics or colours add a cosier touch.

The look: Relax among a seductive mix of colours and textures in an atmosphere of laid-back luxury. Rich pinks and dusky purples are set against contrasting aqua blue walls, while sumptuous soft furnishings sit alongside sleek frosted glass.

Colour: Warm and cool colours blend beautifully here, with walls painted in a muted mid-toned aqua forming a tranquil backdrop for a palette of hot pinks. Keep flooring light – a white carpet is the ultimate luxury – then look for fabrics in a selection of shades, from rich damson to rose pink. Frosted-glass furniture complements the subtle blue walls, while hints of fresh green in cushions and small accessories balance the coordinated look.

Furniture: Frosted-glass furniture has a sophisticated air. The light-reflective glass surface echoes the coolness of the blue walls and white carpet, and these chic metal-framed tables comprise a light touch alongside the large sofa, which is cosily upholstered in a textured weave.

Soft furnishings: Curtains and cushions bring out the sumptuous side of the scheme, so look for sheeny fabrics such as silk and taffeta. To re-create the bloom of plums, dress your window with a double-layered curtain, using sheer organza over rich pink satin in a full-length, heavily gathered style. Continue the effect with a few cushion covers, by making wide-bordered organza covers to slip over pink silk.

Accessories: Hanging a plum-coloured picture in the centre of one wall helps to bring the blue into the scheme. The purple lampshade adds a dark accent which heightens the effect of the duskier plums. Glass vases complement the furniture and add further reflective glamour.

LIVING ROOM TIP
Reflective materials, such as glass, metallics and polished or varnished surfaces, not only add glamorous shine to a room but also bounce light around, making the whole atmosphere seem brighter and airier

The look: If you need a room where you can chill out, then get in perfect harmony with pale shades of blue and lilac. These cool customers will soften the mood in a bright and airy setting to envelop you in an oasis of relaxation.

Colour: The colours we live with can affect us both physically and emotionally. Blue is a calming hue that sharpens the mental faculties, while lilac adds an air of spirituality to a room. So together they create the ideal therapy if you want a peaceful but refreshing environment. Combine pale shades for a thoroughly laid-back mood – try a barely-there lilac on the walls and a slightly deeper lavender and soft china blue for chair covers. Teamed with a plain off-white carpet and curtains, even the lightest colours will shine.

Furniture: Wooden furniture should also be light in tone to avoid overpowering the pale hues. Keep it absolutely simple for an uncluttered feel. Modern tables and units with straight, clean lines are just what you need for a fuss-free look.

Window: The tall window gives the room its airy atmosphere, and the plain curtains play along with that. Their fine white cotton diffuses sunlight to give it a softer quality that suits this relaxing scheme, without lessening its brightening effect on the room.

Accessories: The ethereal mood is enhanced by translucent accessories tinted with pale blue: delicate glassware, a mesh candleholder and a pretty beaded storage box. The TV set adds an accent of darker blue.

The look: A super-wide window floods this room with light, while the coffee and cream colour scheme makes the most of it to provide a bright but relaxing environment. In this spacious atmosphere, the few pieces of modern furniture and accessories take on sculptural qualities.

Colour: Like the furnishings, the colour scheme is beautifully simple, based on a very limited palette of pale neutrals. There is little variation in tone – the carpet, sofa and curtains are all in a similar shade of cream, while the wooden furniture echoes the colour of the walls. Their soft pinky-beige has a calming quality, and its mottled plaster effect adds interest to the plain scheme. It looks like a clever paint finish but is actually a wallpaper – designs that mimic paint effects let you attain these fashionable looks without the stress of added mess.

Furniture: The king-size sofa emphasises the generous proportions of the room, showing how one large item can make a greater impact than several smaller sofas and chairs. Its line-up of white cushions enhances its width, including no colour to break up the effect. When a room has little furniture, what there is must work hard, and the wooden pieces combine cutting-edge shape with storage space and flexibility – the coffee table has a rotating extension, and both tables have wheels for easy manoeuvrability.

Window: Sheer curtains cover the huge window without blocking its light. Although the window ends at dado level, the curtains continue down to the floor for a more decorative effect, and their soft gathers and pretty tie-top heading add a touch of romance to the room.

LIVING ROOM TIP
Check that any sofa you buy will fit through your doors and be able to make its way through narrow hallways or around tight corners before reaching your room. Many manufacturers offer an on-site assembly option for larger styles

The look: In modern rooms, natural textures often find themselves teamed with neutral hues, but this scheme offers a more colourful take on the look. Sun-scorched orange and leafy greens team up with wood and wicker to create an exotic, jungle-like feel.

Colour: Just a step or two away from more earthy shades such as terracotta and olive, the orange and green used here remain in character with the natural theme yet are bright enough to give it a strikingly original look. The walls and curtains form a vibrant contrast, the hot quality of the orange offsetting the freshness of the green. The sandy colours of the furniture and seagrass flooring determine the rustic character of the scheme.

Furniture: Wood and wicker contribute the natural colour and texture which are so important to this look. The bamboo table also adds an oriental touch, in tune with the jungle feel. Covering the sofa in a darker neutral than the other furniture varies the tone, to stop the look from becoming too overpowering.

Window: The blind and curtain combination bring three different shades of green to the scheme. The textured chenille blind, in a pale khaki colour, shades the room from strong sunlight when necessary, while flowing voile curtains in a two-tone stripe bring softness, romance, and zesty colour, to the room.

Accessories: Cushions in silk, raffia and chenille add to the mix of textures, while chunky candles, tall vases and an oriental teapot enhance the oriental feel. Accessories introduce accents of red and pink as well as further splashes of green.

LAID-BACK

The look: A streamlined look for a loft room is what was needed here, and a simple all-yellow colour scheme provides the answer. Shelves and storage units help to keep things neat and tidy.

Colour: Lofts are often on the dark side, but a sunny yellow is guaranteed to brighten things up. With yellow covers and cushions, the sofa seems to disappear against the walls – a great way of increasing the illusion of space. The blind is also yellow, and even the radiator has a matching cover, to create a totally seamless effect. The glowing colour is enhanced by the mellow tones of the beechwood flooring and coffee table.

Furniture: If your aim is a streamlined look, tackling clutter tops the action agenda. Throw out what you can, then look for versatile storage furniture. Drawer units that slot into small spaces and coffee tables with shelves are ideal, and even better if they're on wheels. The cabinet with a raised yellow top provides a double set of surfaces, so one can be used for display – as well as a cat perch!

Shelving: Floor-to-ceiling shelves provide the best form of storage for books and paperwork. To keep things looking tidy, stash them in storage boxes and magazine files before placing on the shelves. Small boxes placed on top of one another make the most of deep shelves.

Accessories: Most accessories stick to the yellow theme, with embroidered cushions bringing texture to the sofa and abstract prints adding interest to the wall above. Accents of silver come from the lamp, pen pot and picture frames.

The look: Energizing yellows and oranges pep up plain whites to create a refreshing, contemporary living-room-cum-study. A table in front of the window provides a working area while blending in with the rest of the furniture.

Colour: Clean whites look bright and modern but can feel clinical if used on their own. Painting the walls in a pale cowslip yellow takes off the chill while enhancing the freshness of the whites. It is complemented by the zesty orange stripes of the curtains, which add a touch of dynamic pattern to the plain scheme. Accents of lime green and lilac add further splashes of contemporary colour.

Furniture: With the floor painted in dazzling white to match the coffee table, the off-white sofa and very pale grey paint finish on the desk give the scheme a little more depth. The chair adds a glimmer of silver that highlights the slick modern feel of the room. If you want a working space that doesn't jar with your decor, resist the temptation to buy an office-style desk and choose a more decorative table instead. This Empire-style console has a couple of useful drawers, but clutter on top is kept to a minimum; fit shelves or cupboards to take care of paperwork and files.

Accessories: A smart metal table lamp lights the desk area, while the green and lilac candles nearby provide stimulating colour rather than illumination. Coloured cushions brighten the sofa, and the print on the wall above reflects all the colours of the scheme as well as the stripes of the curtains. Clear glassware suits the clean, sparkling feel of the room.

The look: Blue is essentially a cool colour, but the strong shades of clear skies create an upbeat, welcoming feel. Keep the atmosphere bright and breezy with pristine white upholstery and simple furniture in blond woods.

Colour: For a really summery atmosphere, paint your walls in shades that pack a punch – using two on different walls helps to break up the effect of the strong colour. Widely varying tones of blue mix beautifully within a room scheme, so include the full range, from baby blues and soft aquas to china and denim shades to deep, dark indigos and navy. The white sofa upholstery and vanilla-coloured carpet lift the look with a dazzling contrast, while the natural tones of the wooden furniture and linen curtains strike a more relaxed note.

Furniture: If you want white or cream upholstery, choose machine-washable loose covers or have fixed fabric treated to protect it from staining. White seating provides the perfect backdrop for an assortment of coloured cushions, while a single chair covered in a big check enlivens the scheme with bold pattern. Simple folding side tables in slatted hardwood give the room an indoor-outdoor dimension.

Soft furnishings: Pile on throws to lift the white sofa with striking bands of blue, and heap up cushions that introduce a diverse mix of texture and pattern. Smart stripes and checks provide a strong contrast with the plain walls.

Window: Natural-coloured linen hung from a pole with wooden finials makes a casual curtain treatment. Get the latest layered look by hanging a simple cotton drape in a crisp stripe from a wire inside the window recess.

The look: Blocks of colour in enough different hues to kit out a rainbow combine with the bold abstract patterns of the rug to give this room a bright, contemporary scheme. Large prints depicting Moroccan street scenes add an exotic feel.

Colour: The aqua wall and navy sofa provide a cool backdrop for the hot reds and oranges of the prints. In turn, their colours are echoed by the multicoloured scatter cushions that lift the dark sofa and in the greens and lilacs of the abstract rug. Splashes of white and cream feature at all levels, in the rug, cushions and the borders of the prints, and they work to freshen and calm the effect created by so many different colours. The ceiling is also painted white to add an impression of height, and this is further enhanced by the effect of the muted flooring.

Furniture: A dark sofa is a practical choice if you're worried about keeping upholstery clean, and you can always dress it with colourful cushions if you want a more cheerful look. Simple wooden side tables look casual and contemporary, and echo the tones of the pine floorboards.

Accessories: As they are contemporary in style, the prints are in tune with the mood of the room, but their subject matter adds an exotic element which is reinforced by the Moroccan-style silk pendant light shade. Modern table lamps with simple white shades provide additional lighting. Placed on either side of the sofa, they bring, along with the two prints and the carefully positioned white cushions, a symmetrical, ordered look to this part of the room.

LAID-BACK

The look: Packed with contemporary colour, this bold scheme shows how two or three powerful shades can not only work together within one room but also flow harmoniously into adjacent spaces, thus avoiding a jarring effect when doors are left open.

Floor: The wood-effect floor provides a neutral base for vibrant colours. If you can't afford solid wood flooring, try cheaper alternatives. Veneered planks have a thin covering of wood laid over a core of chipboard or similar material, while wood-effect laminates are convincing lookalikes.

Colour: The secret behind using bright colour is to team one or two strong shades with more muted tones. Clear contemporary brights such as lime green and violet are at their most stylish when complemented by soft shades such as the raspberry pink of the sofa and the cranberry red of the checked blinds. If these were replaced with a pillarbox red or a shocking pink, the clash would be difficult to live with. On woodwork, off-white is a more sympathetic partner for strongly coloured walls than brilliant white.

Furniture: If you fancy boldly coloured upholstery, ensure it's a colour you love and can live with. Collect large swatches of your chosen fabrics, and observe them in different lights. Loose covers are more versatile than fixed upholstery and are also handy for adding colour to small tables.

Windows: Roller blinds are a wonderfully simple window dressing, ideal for a modern room. They are also great for showing off patterned fabric – these lively checks add pace to a mostly plain room.

LIVING ROOM TIP
Plan your room scheme by making a sample board. Gather paint shade cards, pictures of furniture and swatches of fabric and flooring, then pin them to an A3 sheet of card. This gives you an idea of the overall effect by showing you how patterns and colours work together

The look: Unexpected combinations of furnishings and colours can produce strikingly original looks. Not many people might think of teaming a tartan rug in traditional reds and greens with a sofa upholstered in brilliant contemporary turquoise, but the two provide a stunning contrast that gives real impact to this room.

Colour: Lilac and turquoise is a cool combination, ideal for a chic contemporary setting, but if you want something a bit more exciting, add some bright red – it immediately takes on a more powerful character. The tartan rug and the big scarlet blooms on the cushions cut through the sweetness of the scheme and add some welcome pattern among the clean blocks of plain colour, which can look dull on their own. The natural wood of the shutters glows warmly against the cool lilac walls.

Furniture: The sofa is upholstered in a velvety fabric made up in the form of a loose cover. Button fastenings down the fronts of the arms allow for easy removal when it needs washing, as well as providing an unusual decorative detail. The other chairs have been upholstered in a lighter shade of turquoise that blends effectively with the sofa, while the chunky wooden table reflects the traditional character of the rug.

Window: Shutters show off the shape of the bay window better than curtains. Louvred wooden shutters are a flexible means of light control – their slats can be adjusted to admit as much daylight as possible when they are fully open or provide total blackout when closed, as well as all the degrees in between. They also give a room a stylish, continental look.

The look: Purple and lilac are tops for contemporary chic, and when teamed with white and silver their slick glamour really shines through. Sumptuous soft furnishings and flickering candlelight complement the colours for a glittering, luxurious look.

Colour: White paintwork on the skirting and shelving provides a fresh contrast for the intense lilac on the walls. As well as the touches of silver that feature in accessories, the scheme is enriched by accent colours of hot pink, turquoise and purple, introduced mainly in the cushions.

Furniture: Alcoves beside the fireplace are convenient storage spaces, and built-in cupboard and shelf units make full use of them. Draping the sofa in a light blue throw updates it to fit the scheme. A second throw in lilac velvet and a selection of similarly luxurious cushion fabrics make for sumptuous seating.

Screen: The screen behind the sofa conceals a 1970s-style archway. Stylish screens can be expensive but it doesn't take much DIY skill to make your own. Screw together lengths of 44 x 44mm timber to form a frame. To fill the frame, use lengths of sheer or metallic fabric, fixing them to the wood with drawing pins or furniture tacks. Make three or four panels and hinge them together.

Accessories: Silver accessories that glam up the scheme include the shiny tealight holder and the galvanised boxes stacked on the shelves. Storage boxes are a neat way of housing paperwork and smaller items, to prevent shelf units from looking messy. Sparkling candles are an essential finishing touch for this romantic look.

LIVING ROOM TIP
It can be difficult to find throws that completely cover a large sofa, but ready-made curtain panels or bedspreads do the job just as well

The look: This scheme sets off the classic-style features of a Victorian room with a relaxing palette of soft, contemporary neutrals. Sheer fabrics and wax treatments give window dressings and furniture a light touch to create a look of effortless elegance.

Colour: The toffee colour on the walls tones closely with the wooden floorboards to create a warm atmosphere, while cool cream contrasts make for neutral chic. Animal-print cushions enrich the simple scheme with dashes of striking pattern, and add black accents to echo the fireplace.

Furniture: The Art Deco chair has had its wooden frame treated with liming wax and its original leatherette upholstery replaced with white cotton, to match the sofa cover. The elegant coffee table is a bargain creation made from a plastic wood-effect planter topped with a sheet of glass.

Window: Lush classic-style curtains get a modern twist when made from sheer fabrics. Using light-diffusing muslin means you can have generously gathered drapes without darkening the room, and it's a lot cheaper than most heavier materials. This bay window is layered with panels of cream and caramel muslin gathered onto curtain wire. A natural tea dye gives the caramel panels their colour – dip cream muslin into a brew of about 100 tea bags infused in water, for an hour.

Accessories: Old-fashioned prints hanging by chains from the picture rail bring out the classic style of the room, while zebra-print cushions add a touch of contemporary glamour. Candles provide mood lighting – elaborate wrought-iron candlesticks embelish the fireplace, while the terracotta pots on the coffee table make simple cut-price holders.

LIVING ROOM TIP
Reinstating architectural features such as picture and dado rails helps to restore the original proportions of a period room. They are also useful for adding character to plain, boxy rooms in modern houses

The look: With its antique-style leather sofa and collection of prints and family portraits, this room has the distinguished air of a gentlemen's club.

Colour: A gutsy green provides a bold contrast for both the chestnut tones of the sofa and the lighter yellows, whites and golds of the framed prints. It's a shade that's rich but not sombre – deep enough to give a strongly traditional feel but also cheerful enough for a family room.

Furniture: There's nothing like old leather if you want to give your scheme the stamp of cosy tradition. It's tough as old boots and keeps on improving with age, so a second-hand or antique sofa is a good investment. Team it with chunky furniture in woods that tone with the leather; in today's living rooms old trunks are finding a new, more decorative role as casual coffee or side tables, while still fulfilling their function of providing ample storage.

Lighting: A single pendant lamp intended to provide general illumination remains the favourite form of lighting for many of us, but using light more creatively can make a real difference to the mood of a room. A pair of lamps hung low over the coffee table bathes it in soft pools of light, giving the seating area a more intimate air and also making the shapely shades into more of a feature.

Accessories: A group of pictures arranged gallery-style on a wall has greater impact than just one or two in isolation. Leafy plants complement the green walls, while brightly patterned cushions add accents of orange, yellow and black.

LIVING ROOM TIP
To keep leather furniture clean and supple, dust it regularly and rub the surface occasionally with hide food. Keep it away from radiators and open fires, which will dry it out

The look: The palest tones of cream and sage green create a soothing atmosphere that's elegantly subtle. It's a cool but comfortable look, with cosy knitted throws and textured furnishings adding a hint of natural warmth.

Colour: In a room that looks out over a garden, decorating with green appears to bring the natural world inside. The tranquil sage spreads shades of foliage across the walls, but it is cream that dominates the room, keeping the overall look light rather than rustic, and giving a modern edge to the traditional character of the green. Apart from the merest hint of pattern and tinges of pale green in the two cushions, only the subtlest of neutral tones and natural textures vary the uniformity of the scheme.

Texture: With a restrained colour scheme and a minimum of pattern, it falls to textured surfaces to provide the visual interest that any room needs. The carpet has a tiny chequerboard design, the sofa fabric incorporates a self-patterned stripe and the knitted throw adds its ribbed texture and plushy brown velvet border to the mix. The lidded seagrass storage basket also provides natural woven texture.

Furniture: A modern sofa with clean lines effortlessly fits in with the simplicity of the colour scheme. The more decorative console table, with curly brass drawer handles, introduces a touch of traditional style and elegance. Classic furniture in white or cream sits well among more contemporary surroundings, so if you have wooden pieces with attractive old-fashioned shapes, painting can be an effective way of bringing them up to date.

The look: With looks borrowed from a stately home, this scheme takes its inspiration from the traditional bookcases and armchair. The room is split into two parts: a 'library', complete with mock wood panelling on the walls, is kept distinct from the sitting area by a newly created archway.

Colour: Cream paintwork keeps the overall look light and spacious, to offset the darkening effect of the wall-to-wall bookcases. The sofas and armchairs combine a restrained mix of blues, greys and cream with bolder checks. A hint of warmer colour is introduced by the beige carpet.

Arch: The arch dividing the room is made from MDF and hardboard, built into a curved shape across the ceiling with plinths at either side. Resting on the plinths are candlesticks made from banister spindles.

Walls: The panelled look in the library is created by painting the walls with brown emulsion, followed by a mixture of magnolia emulsion and scumble glaze, which is then grained using a special tool to give a wood effect. Strips of lining paper, painted to match, are glued on top to create imitation panelling. The other walls are painted with a grid effect to resemble stone blocks. A mural in the style of an 18th-century landscape forms a focal point in the sitting area.

Furniture: A small chipboard table painted with a scroll and leaf design adds a colourful touch amid the dark wood and upholstered furniture. At the far end of the sitting area, a decorative screen conceals the TV set.

LIVING ROOM TIP
TV and audio equipment often looks out of place, especially in a period-style room. A screen will conceal that jumble of technology but a neater option is a specially made cabinet, with doors that open for easy viewing and a gap in the back to let cables pass through

The look: Go green in a big way, and combine the fresh shades of summer foliage in a patchwork of wall squares. The elegant curves and flowing leaf patterns of classic-style furniture soften the bold geometry of the checks.

Colour: For an uplifting effect, select your wall colours from the fresh side of the green palette. Choose a range of shades, from pale salad hues and tangy lime to verdant grassy greens. White woodwork creates a clean border, freshening the look further. The beige carpet and traditional greens of the upholstered furniture act as a calming influence.

Walls: In a room with large areas of wall, breaking them up with checks adds an extra dimension. Using a plumbline and spirit level, measure up and draw out your checks on the wall, ending with complete squares at the top and sides. Before masking off and painting them, make a plan on paper showing which colours should go where so that you get a pleasing, random effect. A few squares in this room are stencilled with a fern design.

Furniture: The classic-style furniture contrasts with the lively modern wall treatment in terms of style, shape and colour. The sofa and chair are upholstered in relaxing shades of sage, while the footstool and cushions feature delicate fern patterns, which join with the curvaceous design of the furniture to offset the straight lines of the squares.

Accessories: A sheer white panel at the window keeps the look crisp, as do clear glass accessories, such as the lampbase and candlesticks. Real foliage, in pot plants and floral displays, brings a green scheme to life.

The look: With its rustic overtones, olive green makes a compatible partner for the wooden furniture and fire surround, and complements the battered elegance of an old leather chaise and coffee table trunk to give this room its cosy traditional feel.

Colour: The gentle shade of green on the walls gives the room a relaxing atmosphere that blends comfortably with the nostalgic character of the furniture. The floorboards continue the sombre traditional scheme with their covering of green and black satin-finish paint. Decorating the woodwork in cream gives a softer contrast than fresh white.

Fireplace: The fire surround, which was picked up at a salvage yard, has been stripped and stained a teak colour to give it a finish that blends with the wooden furniture in the room.

Window: Wooden Venetian blinds fit in with the other natural furnishings and also have a practical advantage in that they let plenty of light flow between their slats when open, to brighten the atmosphere.

Furniture: The furniture includes a mixture of family heirlooms and junk-shop finds, which each add their own character but come together to create a relaxed, lived-in look. The curves of the wooden chair and chaise add attractive shape to the scheme, while the glass front of the cabinet reflects light from the windows. Cushions and throws in muted colours are draped over the chaise and coffee table trunk to add decorative pattern and conceal any shabbiness of the furniture.

LIVING ROOM TIP
Remember that light can affect colours dramatically. A shade may change many times throughout the day and will also look different under artificial light. Buy sample pots to try out paint colours on your wall, and view them under all conditions before making your choice

The look: This room is a melting pot for a mixture of old and new furniture and fabrics. Clever use of colour makes them work successfully together to create an easy-to-live-with look that's full of character.

Colour: The buttermilk shade on the walls bridges the gap between the contemporary creams and greens of the sofa and cushions and the rich golds and browns of the curtains and floral chair. While toning beautifully with the latter, it also shares the freshness of the lighter colours, complementing both the old and new elements of the room. Using the cream in large blocks, for the sofa and rug, ensures that the overall look remains light, while lime green sharpens it up with zestier colour.

Furniture: Many of us own an eclectic collection of furniture, and there's no reason why wildly diverse pieces shouldn't share room space. Individual items can result in a far more interesting look than a coordinated set, so bring that old wooden furniture down from the attic and see how it looks alongside your modern sofa, colourful coffee table and inflatable plastic pouffe!

Window: The curtains really are an attic find – the owner's grandmother had them hidden away – but as the fabric is in good nick they have found a new lease of life. If you want to save money on curtains, but aren't handy with a sewing machine, second-hand bargains could be the answer.

Floor: The floor is covered with cork tiles, half of which are dyed to create a chequerboard effect. Several coats of polyurethane varnish keep this budget flooring looking as good as new.

The look: Bring a little timeless romance into your living room with a look inspired by grand aristocratic residences. Sparkling chandeliers, delicate toile patterns and elegantly distressed furniture are the key ingredients of French château style.

Colour: For an airy, feminine feel, choose a pretty pastel wall colour such as pale yellow. Keep the look light with cream furniture, and cover your floorboards with a rug if they look too rustic. Layer patterned fabrics to introduce additional colour: faded florals, subtle stripes and dainty sprigs all add up to a blissfully romantic look, but the essential print is toile de Jouy. Patterned with traditional pastoral scenes, it comes in a range of colours on a white background.

Furniture: Search for graceful furniture with curved lines and a slightly battered appearance – distressed pieces create that comfortably lived-in feel. This is an easy look to create on a budget as you can use paint effects to distress junk-shop bargains or cheap MDF blanks. A focal point in this room is the beautifully painted screen that conceals the black fireplace. The sofa is also hidden, beneath a fringed and embroidered throw.

Windows: Minimal dressings suit modern rooms, but for classic elegance windows should be dressed. These toile de Jouy curtains are fully lined and hang down to the floor for a luxurious feel. Iron poles with curly metal finials are perfectly in character.

Accessories: Candlelight and chandeliers spell romance – this one is made from an old wire planter with tea lights bound onto it. Gold details, such as the gilt mirror frame, also exude period glamour.

LIVING ROOM TIP
Look for antique textiles in charity shops, markets and car boot sales, where they can often be picked up cheaply. Used as sofa throws and table runners, lacy and embroidered fabrics are wonderful for adding a whiff of old-time charm

The look: If you want to give your living room a warmer, more welcoming feel but don't relish bold colour on your walls, then try the palest tint of yellow. Teamed with soft oranges and browns, it will create a relaxing but welcoming environment.

Colour: The walls are decorated with paper in a pale cowslip yellow that tones with the blond wood of the floor. White woodwork punctuates this delicate backdrop. The furniture provides stronger colour in the form of natural materials – tan-coloured leather and the warm browns of bamboo and rattan. An orange chenille rug adds comfort and colour to the floor, while toning with the leather chair. Yellow cushions and accessories strengthen the effect of the wall colour by introducing brighter accents.

Furniture: Leather chairs look at home in many different settings, and the oriental-look furniture now on sale in many high-street stores is equally versatile. Here these two styles sit side by side, adding a blend of natural browns to the colour scheme. They each bring their own distinctive shape to the room, the delicate lines of the rattan table contrasting with the comfortable curves of the chair.

Accessories: The oriental feel introduced by the rattan table is reinforced by a selection of accessories: the bamboo-framed mirror on the wall is particularly evocative, while the dark wood lampbase and candleholders and the sisal basket also suggest ethnic or eastern style. Other items – the radio, cushions and candles in a dish – add splashes of yellow and orange.

The look: Fruity shades of lemon, tangerine and watermelon pink come together in this deliciously colourful scheme. The inspiration is classic, with Regency stripes on soft furnishings and metal curlicues on furniture, but quirky elements such as the animal-print rug and cushions add individual style.

Colour: The bold yellow walls blend with wood flooring in a similar shade to create an atmosphere of all-round warmth. This is continued by the foreground sofa, which features a subtle stripe combining closely toning hues of pink and orange. The cream and pink striped sofa gives the scheme a more delicate, feminine look which is enhanced by a couple of floral cushions. In contrast, the animal-print furnishings add accents of black which are echoed by the picture frame. Other cushions, appliquéd with naive designs, reflect the colour of the walls.

Furniture: Large and richly upholstered sofas epitomise classic style, so this big pink and white version with its striped and figured fabric exudes old-world elegance. The look is reinforced by the metal bookshelf with spiral decorations and the pretty brass wall lamps hung with crystal droplets. The nest tables have curves that are in keeping, but have been updated with bright colour. Each table is painted in a different shade to add another fun touch to the room.

Window: Classic luxury demands generous swathes of curtain fabric. For true period style, lavishly gathered drapes should be held back at the sides with tiebacks, and are often embellished with swags and tails at the top. These full-length curtains with smart raspberry and cream stripes look suitably dramatic.

The look: Deep pink adds punch to the country-cottage look, providing a vibrant contrast for cream-coloured furnishings and delicate floral patterns.

Colour: If you love pretty prints and feminine pinks but don't want a look that's too girly, use pattern only in tiny amounts and strengthen the look with bold colour contrasts. Hot pink is an excellent foil for cool cream. As well as creating greater impact, it will give your room a warmer, more intimate feel than a pale shade. By virtue of contrast, it also allows the subtlest of patterns to shine; the pale pinks of the pictures might fade into a lighter background but here are highlighted against the vibrant wall. The floral cushion is also delicately patterned – this is no place for brash chintzes that might fight with the wall colour.

Furniture: To get the full effect of the colour contrast, choose cream-coloured furniture. Textured fabric will add interest to sofas and chairs upholstered in plain shades. Team them with tables and chests made from wood or with a cream-painted finish.

Pictures: The pictures you hang on your wall don't have to be works of art – the simplest designs can add pattern and colour. This display consists of wallpaper samples, shown off in customized frames. Prime wooden frames with white paint, then apply a soft pink. Rub over the dry surface with a warm candle and add a top coat or two of cream-coloured paint. When the final coat is dry, sand lightly to reveal highlights of the pink beneath. To finish, buff with furniture polish.

The look: Green is easy on the eye and easy to use: a harmonising colour that you can play around with to create a setting either of apple freshness or lush serenity. Traditional or country-style interiors look good in softer shades complemented by natural wood tones and simple flower and leaf patterns.

Colour: Lighter greens create an atmosphere that's both relaxing and refreshing – use shade upon shade together and they will look stunning. This room combines a classic pistachio on the walls with furniture painted in grassier greens and a fresh-toned sofa. The wooden flooring warms up the look and brings out the natural quality of the greens, while dashes of white and cream add a lighter contrast.

Pattern: Based on the colour of nature, a green scheme lends itself perfectly to floral and leaf prints. For a subtle air of country charm, choose two-tone designs with small or clearly defined motifs, rather than busy, multicoloured prints. The sofa is covered with a spriggy white-on-green design, while the curling leaf sprays of the curtain pattern are in an understated, earthy shade that echoes the flooring and chair.

Furniture: Traditional-style furniture and decorative pieces with scalloped edging or curvy contours add shape and detail to a room. Look for wooden chairs or tables that blend with the tones of your flooring, or paint others green to match the scheme. Some companies sell furniture 'blanks' made from unfinished wood, which come ready to paint. Other pieces may need preparation, such as sanding or stripping off varnish, before paint will adhere.

The look: If it's rustic appeal you're after, go for beiges, browns and greens, with natural flooring and layers of texture. Pale walls give the look an elegant edge, while cosy soft furnishings add old-fashioned comfort.

Colour: The cream-painted walls create a clean, plain background that lifts the whole room. For a traditional feel, develop the scheme with darker or muted greens such as olive or deep leafy shades, teamed with browns and greys in varying tones.

Texture: The rustic look relies on texture, so introduce it wherever possible – in natural flooring and furniture as well as woven or knitted fabrics. Even smaller accessories, such as the ribbed lamp with cane shade, can be valuable texture bearers. For this cosy look, mix rough surfaces with plenty of soft fabrics.

The patchwork lambswool throw adds warmth and comfort as well as a home-crafted country feel.

Furniture: Chairs and sofas can be any style provided they look cosy. Choose upholstery with a textured weave, then pile on throws and cushions to boost the snuggle factor. Ethnic furniture in wicker, rattan or other woven materials suits the textured look – here a basketweave chest doubles as a coffee table – but use it in moderation unless you want to pursue an oriental theme.

Lighting: In any living room, table and standard lamps are essential sources of task lighting – they illuminate leisure pursuits such as reading or sewing. Include lamps of varying heights in styles that suit your scheme: the textured lamp enhances the rustic mood, while the standard lamp reflects the elegant side of the look.

The look: The elaborate black ironwork and floral hearth tiles of this room's Victorian fireplace are offset by a plain, almost rustic style of decor based on white walls and wood tones. The old Indian table, wooden shutters and animal prints add a slightly colonial air.

Colour: The walls are painted in chalky off-white, forming a plain foil for a varied collection of furniture and accessories. Apart from the black fireplace, which stands out strongly against the walls, woody browns predominate in the tones of the stripped floorboards and furniture. Green accents add spots of colour while keeping the theme natural.

Furniture: Wooden furniture with character enhances a room's period charm, even though its origins may be very different. The coffee table comes from India where it was designed as a child's bed, while the wooden trolley was rescued from a skip on a London street. Different upholstery for each sofa gives a more individual look than a matching set A leopard-print seat cover and green cushions enliven the white sofa.

Window: Full-length shutters do the job of curtains. As well as making simple and stylish treatments for a large window, they add to the wood tones in the room. Voile hung café-style over the bottom half of the windows gives privacy during the day.

Accessories: Wicker baskets provide storage beneath the trolley and table. Like other accessories, such as the woven light shade and terracotta pot, they add natural colour and texture. Plants and foliage both reinforce and freshen the rustic atmosphere.

The look: A moody mixture of grey-toned aqua and rich plum, plus layers of soft-textured furnishings, make this room into a real comfort zone. The unexpected colour combination and dark furniture give the scheme a formal, sophisticated look.

Colour: Plum and aubergine create a luxurious feel; drape a deep-toned sofa with throws and cushions in similar shades and smoky greys to put the emphasis on comfort. Plum can be overpowering if used throughout a room, but cool aqua mellows the look. Muted tones keep the mood soft: two subtle shades feature in the wallpaper. The stripes focus interest on the aqua, helping it to balance the strong purples. Splashes of fresh white, in the rug and fireplace, give a lift to the scheme.

Floor: For a really cosy atmosphere, choose a dark floorcovering. It will make your room feel smaller, but also more intimate. This blue cord blends with the rich tones of the furniture to enhance the moody atmosphere.

Furniture: Indulge yourself with sumptuous textures when dressing your sofa. This one is upholstered in velvet and piled with a mohair throw and cushions in silk, velvet and wool. A plum-coloured leather chair boosts the sophistication and provides a smooth contrast for the soft fabrics. Dark wood furniture tones well with deep colours. If you're afraid it might seem too heavy, choose a glass-fronted cabinet for a more open look.

Accessories: As aqua features only on the walls, accessories can help to bring it into the rest of the room. Include tableware and vases in both plum and aqua, plus a little glassware for a glamorous touch.

LIVING ROOM TIP
Buy all your wallpaper in one go, as batches may vary slightly in colour. Calculate carefully how much you'll need for the whole room, but always get one roll more than you reckon on, just in case!

The look: Perfect symmetry and a vista through a succession of broad doorways bring a grand sense of space and proportion to an average-sized suburban bungalow.

Colour: If you have a view through two or more rooms, pick a mix of colours that flows smoothly; the trick is to choose ones similar in tone. Here a selection of clear mid-tones teams well: a rosy lilac in the sitting room gives way to mint green in the dining room and aqua blue beyond. The door frames are white throughout to provide a visual link. Different carpeting helps give each room its own character – a deep blue pile carpet sets the tone for comfort in the living room.

Glass doors: Internal doors with glass panels look more attractive and less imposing than a solid material. The glass reflects light and, even with the doors closed, allows it to flow freely through the house.

Furniture: Chairs upholstered in gold velvet add to the air of luxury. Chocolate scatter cushions echo the dark wood of the coffee table to give the room a coordinated look. The layout also spells order: everything is arranged symmetrically around the line running through the doorways – even down to the two urns on plinths beside the window and the pot plants guarding the entrance.

Shelving: Fitted wall shelves emphasise the symmetry and provide country-manor-style storage for books. The alcoves on either side provide display space for classic-style wall lamps and ornaments.

The look: Modern furniture sits comfortably with this room's Victorian features. The merest hint of blue adorns the walls in an ice-cool scheme warmed by the natural tones of wood and wicker.

Colour: The pale forget-me-not shade on the walls results from adding a dash of blue to white emulsion, and is designed to make the room feel cosier while keeping the overall effect bright. The ceiling and walls above the picture rail are painted in off-white, with the rail itself picked out in brilliant white. The black Victorian fireplace stands out smartly against the pale walls, and the blue chair balances it with another dark tone. The rug adds further shades of blue but it is used in moderation, allowing the stripped wood flooring to set a light but relaxed mood.

Furniture: A tub chair looks at home in both traditional and modern rooms. The wicker table adds natural texture that tones with the pine floorboards. The wood-framed screen offers an original way of displaying family photos, while mono-chrome pictures complement the black and white contrasts in the room.

Window: Solid shutters are a neat but efficient method of screening the small window. Their natural pine echoes the floorboards and their old-fashioned appeal blends with the original features of the room. A sheer curtain provides privacy during the daytime.

Accessories: Wicker pots and magazine files add further natural interest, while the classic lamp, candleholders and fireguard pay homage to the room's Victorian origins.

The look: Sunny yellow walls cast their glow over a mixture of contemporary and traditional furniture, including the shapely Art Deco armchair that makes a strong feature in one corner of the room.

Colour: Brilliant yellow is not only a warm, feelgood colour, but it also reflects natural light from the windows to create a bright sun-kissed atmosphere at any time of year. Teaming it with wood enhances the feeling of warmth, whether it's the mellow tones of the coffee table and flooring or the richer grain of the chair and trunk. Cream and green, the other colours of the scheme, represent its two different faces: the cream blinds and sofa give a light, modern look, while dark green evokes a more traditional feel, the foliage of the plants reflecting the upholstery of the armchair.

Furniture: The Art Deco chair is a 1930s put-you-up that converts into a single bed. Beside it is an old wooden trunk that doubles as a display area. Musical instruments add character and a personal touch to this traditional corner. The sofa, with its loosely fitting cream cover, also converts to a bed. When it does so, the wheeled coffee table can easily be whisked out of the way.

Windows: Roller blinds make plain and simple dressings for both the tiny window and the French doors. Buy a kit from curtain or department stores that includes all the fixtures and fittings, plus instructions, and you'll find roller blinds easy to put together.

The look: There's no need to chuck out everything in a room and start from scratch – the lived-in look makes the most of your favourite bits of furniture. A traditional leather chair, an old garden table and granny's hand-me-down coffee table are all laden with character, and just one old piece will make a new scheme out of the ordinary.

Colour: A plain backdrop is the perfect foil for a variety of furnishings, and a classic shade of rich cream creates an atmosphere that's light and space-friendly but also comfortable. Let your old furniture dictate the rest of your colour scheme – here, the red-toned leather of the armchair is balanced by the equally dark blue of the sofa. Patterned cushions add accents that echo the gold and orange tones of the coffee table and floorboards.

Furniture: The key to this look is worn in not worn out – what you want is furniture that looks as if it has a history. Junk and antiques shops are excellent sources, but you could also try the high street for new pieces made to look distressed. The easy-living theme thrives on an eclectic mix of furniture – this leather armchair is joined by an antique French garden table and a second-hand bamboo coffee table. The style also calls for lots of lounging, so add a comfy sofa piled with cushions in a variety of fabrics. Wooden and wicker trunks provide casual forms of storage.

Window: Separate roller blinds side by side make a versatile window treatment as they can be raised or lowered individually. They are made from semi-sheer, self-striped cream linen and edged with taupe-coloured linen scrim.

LIVING ROOM TIP
If you want a convincing classic-style colour scheme, search out the heritage ranges now offered by several paint companies. These are based on original colours used in authentic period homes

The look: A rambling stencil gives these walls the look of expensive handpainted wallpaper. Applied in a cool blue over a neutral base, it creates an elegant backdrop for either traditional or contemporary furnishings.

Colour: Stencils in garish colours are a key to disaster, so stick to soft shades if you want to ensure a chic look. If you choose a busy pattern, keep the rest of your colour scheme plain and simple. The powdery blue and off-white used on these walls are repeated in the shades of the fireplace, chair cover and accessories. Add accents in other colours to lift the look, but don't overdo them: the flowers and throw introduce splashes of purple and lilac.

Wall stencil: If stencils call to mind grapevines and ivy trails, take another look – today's designs are much more sophisticated. Specialist stencil suppliers offer hundreds to choose from, as well as all the paints and equipment you need to apply them. For an all-over design like this, you will need to buy a repeat stencil. If your walls are uneven, fill in any cracks, then hang lining paper to give them a smooth finish and paint this with your base colour. For a speedier, even finish when applying the stencil design, use a tiny sponge roller instead of a brush.

Furniture: The traditional-style armchair complements the character of the old-fashioned floral stencil design. You could continue the look with elegant white-painted tables or chests of drawers.

Accessories: An embroidered bag enhances the delicate feel of the scheme, but vases and tableware have clean modern shapes to offset the highly patterned walls.

The look: Keep that carefree holiday feel all year round with a vibrant modern scheme inspired by the colours of a summer beach. The deep blue of a cloudless sky covers the walls, while pale upholstery and unfinished wood are reminiscent of a sun-bleached driftwood effect.

Colour: The brilliant contrast between the deep blue walls and cream sofa conjures up images of tropical skies and white sandy beaches. It is tempered by the neutral tones of the marble fireplace, oak laminate flooring and wooden furniture, which also carry echoes of the natural world. The exotic tropical feel is underlined by the use of glowing rainbow colours as accents in the window panels, pink chair cover and striped cushions.

Furniture: The traditional curves and cushioned comfort of the large sofa contrast with the basic lines and construction of the wooden tables. Made of rough, unfinished timber nailed together in the style of a seaside boardwalk, they keep the tone casual, offsetting the rather imposing fireplace.

Window: The window is hung with sheer linen panels, each one dyed a different colour. Craft and haberdashery stores sell dyes that can be applied either by hand or in the washing machine. They come in many shades, but remember that the final result depends on the original colour of your fabric. For the best results, dye white or cream materials made of natural fibres.

Accessories: The seascape picture links the room with its inspiration, and the twiggy lampbase resembles a bunch of driftwood. Lighten the impact of the strong colours by reintroducing them in smaller glass accessories.

The look: The cutting-edge decor in this large loft-style space is inspired by a gallery of modern art. Bold geometric blocks of colour contrast with the soft curves of a specially made seating area, while a sculptural paving-stone and perspex coffee table forms an intriguing centrepiece.

Colour: White walls create a blank canvas for the dynamic blocks of colour painted on to look like works of art. The colours are from test pots of emulsion, which save buying larger cans if you need only small amounts. Silver leaf, applied in squares above the sofa, adds a touch of glitz, and echoes the metallic greys of the stones in the coffee table. The concrete floor is painted in a sandy shade that tones with the hardboard of the sofa unit.

Sofa: The dramatic curved sofa breaks up the rectangular shape of the room, and its back panel screens off a dining area. It is made from hardboard nailed onto a timber frame, and the foam seat pad is covered with white cotton. Jewel-coloured scatter cushions make the unit look and feel more comfortable.

Perspex screen: Behind the dining area, a rippling Perspex screen conceals the entrance to the kitchen. Made by stapling clear corrugated Perspex onto S-shaped MDF supports, it is sprayed with white paint to give an opaque look and futuristic feel.

Coffee table: The paving-stone coffee table is reminiscent of a controversial modern sculpture. The trail of concrete paving slabs across the floor culminates in a mound of loosely piled stones with a piece of Perspex screwed to the top one. It makes a shaky table – but an instant conversation piece!

LIVING ROOM TIP
Change the look of your home as often as your wardrobe – stretch canvas panels over wooden frames, then paint and hang instead of pictures. Keep the walls neutral and simply repaint the panels when you fancy a change

The look: Taking the sleek Japanese coffee table as its starting point, this scheme follows through the oriental influence with clean, contemporary styling. However, it rejects the all-out austerity of Japanese minimalism in favour of a palette of beautiful blues and soothing touches such as floaty organza curtains.

Colour: While pared-down oriental rooms are usually based on monochrome tones, cool blues give this large space a more comfortable and colourful look. The walls are livened up with a stencilled border of squares, which echo the cream and white paintwork of the coving and ceiling. The floorboards, painted with a white woodstain and finished with gloss varnish, keep the look light, while the blue sofas strengthen it with a darker tone.

Furniture: Low futon-style sofas team with the straight lines of the coffee table to form the most overtly oriental elements of the scheme, but squashy cushions add an air of comfort.

Window: Wooden-framed shutters covered with cream-coloured cotton create a neat dressing for the large window. Glamorous sheer curtains made from blue organza and edged with a silver border are a purely decorative addition, and are used in an original way, to cover the adjacent walls rather than the window.

Accessories: The oriental feel is enhanced by a large pot of dried twigs and a huge scented candle sitting on blocks of timber. Test-tubes hung from the ceiling with thin wire make contemporary vases for sprays of white lilies. An unusual chandelier made from a blue glass bowl fixed into a frame of MDF is another strikingly modern touch.

The look: Polish up your act with glowing metallics, and bring the look of luxury to your home. With sheeny, shiny fabrics and one or two shimmering accessories, you can be surrounded by riches for next to nothing. Balance just a few items with softer textures and complementary colours for all the impact your room needs.

Colour: Don't overdo the Midas touch or your home will end up looking more brass tacks than gold standard. Paint your walls in a light neutral shade, such as white or cream, and keep your flooring and large pieces of furniture free of glitz. This room grounds the scheme with dark brown floorboards and a chocolate-coloured sofa. Add shimmering soft furnishings in shades of gold and light brown, and accent your plain walls with one or two vertical strips of gold paper.

Soft furnishings: For a metallic effect, choose light-reflective fabrics such as silks and organza to make blinds and cushions. If you want a contemporary feel, keep your window dressings simple, but pile your sofa with glamourously covered cushions to emphasise the air of luxury.

Furniture: The deep brown of the large and comfy sofa provides a rich contrast with the glimmering cushions. Use smaller pieces of furniture to increase the metallic factor – a squirt of gold spray paint makes a small side table look like a million dollars.

Accessories: Picture frames, vases and tableware all offer the opportunity to add glitz without overdoing it. Decorate a frame with gold leaf, and search the high street stores for gleaming accessories that look a lot more expensive than they are.

LIVING ROOM TIP
Add glittering effects to accessories using metallic leaf. Real gold and silver leaf is expensive but metallic alternatives look just as glitzy. Craft stores sell gilding kits complete with the special glue and brushes that you need

The look: Switch on to reds, oranges and yellows for a truly fiery atmosphere. This sizzling contemporary scheme uses wall-to-wall colour to turn up the temperature.

Colour: Hot shades will cosy up the chilliest room. Using them throughout maximizes the illusion of warmth, but beware – they also make a room seem smaller, and may feel over-stimulating if you prefer a restful environment. The natural colours of fire and flame – sunny yellows, burnt oranges and radiant reds – work well together in this room. Toning vertical stripes on the walls blend with an orange carpet and sofa. The skirting board is decorated in metallic gold paint, and even the accessories continue the colour theme.

Wall stripes: With roughly blended edges, the wall stripes create a flame-like effect. Measure your wall and divide it into equal sections, using chalk to mark on lines. Paint the first stripe, then move on to the next before the first is fully dry so the colours merge slightly where they meet. Use a large 10 or 12cm paintbrush for best results.

Furniture: Modern furniture complements the bold colours to give a striking contemporary look, with the sleek silver frames of the tables highlighted against the rich backdrop. The chair is colour themed with a yellow loose cover, and the sofa is stacked with cushions in cosy materials such as mohair.

Accessories: Bring the fiery theme alive with plenty of flickering candles and a groovy lava lamp. The candle flames are reflected in the glass accessories and tabletop.

The look: This smart look is inspired by tailored suiting, with the sofa in navy pinstripe wool setting the tone. The wall behind is painted with a checked design in broken lines to look like tailor's chalk.

Colour: A sophisticated colour scheme in plain neutrals complements the business-like appeal of the scheme. The walls are painted in a warm shade of camel which is just dark enough to show up the white dotted lines. Flooring and furniture in blond wood blend with the wall shade to keep the look light and modern. As the only area of colour among the neutral furnishings, the navy sofa is the focal point. Its pinstripes join with the wall checks to enliven the plain look with an element of pattern.

Texture: The varied textures of the curtains, cushions and throw also prevent the scheme from seeming dull. The long curtains are made from cream corduroy, the throw has a ridged design and the cushions are made from a mix of linen and woven fabrics.

Furniture: Functional furniture with contemporary lines suits the mood of the room, while the rattan panel of the tall cupboards adds a slightly more relaxed feel. The coffee table is made from a cube of foam glued to a piece of MDF fitted with castors. The bouclé cover gives it a designer finish and adds another texture to the mix of soft furnishings.

Accessories: The modern lamp, ashtray and vase all introduce gentle curves, which contrast with the straight lines of the furniture and the formal geometry of the checks and stripes.

The look: There's nothing understated about this room, where a palette of bold contemporary colours combines with decorative painted furniture and classic-style wrought-iron accessories to create a highly individual look.

Colour: To create an extravagant rainbow effect, choose a medley of colours, each as brilliant as the next, and use them on different walls. The brightest shades of fuchsia, saffron and sky blue cheer up this Victorian room, and the riot of colour continues with the deep blues used on the furniture. Only the white skirting board, natural floorcovering and wooden picture and mirror frames provide more sober touches.

Furniture: Chosen more for looks than comfort, an old garden bench makes an unusual and eye-catching 'sofa'. Like the scallop-edged coffee table, it has been transformed with bright blue paint. The sunray-style spokes on its curved back are picked out in a lighter shade of blue, and pink spots along the front edge echo the wall colour behind. To paint wooden furniture, first sand it down to provide a key, then apply a few coats of gloss or satinwood followed by protective varnish for a hard-wearing finish.

Cushions: A collection of cushions turns the wooden bench into a cosier seating experience. The colours and designs of the simple tie-fastened covers match the walls for boldness, with the sharp lime green singing out against the dark blue bench.

Accessories: Wrought-iron candleholders and lampstands offset the modern blocks of colour with a flourish of spirals and scrolls. Underneath the bench, a galvanized tub containing twig balls indicates its rustic origins.

LIVING ROOM TIP
If you are painting adjacent walls in different colours, paint the lighter colour first. It will be easier to cut in with the darker shade at the corners where the colours meet

The look: Checks and stripes, the smart classics of the pattern world, have an especially crisp feel when used in blue and white. Stripes can be low key and casual or regimental and business-like, while the universal appeal of checks lies in their simplicity.

Colour: The far wall features a checked design, with big squares in four shades of blue – a great effect when used on just one or two walls. Together with the indigo table cover, these toning shades create a moody backdrop for the fresh blue and white fabrics of the chairs and cushions.

Pattern: If you base your scheme on checks and stripes, vary the sizes of the designs for an effect that's easy on the eye. Try covering a number of chairs with individually patterned fabrics rather than coordinating prints. Striped ticking has classic appeal – add cushions in plains and simple checks to break up the regimented look. Used in moderation, a spriggy floral-print fabric helps to soften the bold geometry.

Furniture: Loose covers are a good way of adding pattern or colour to existing furniture. Make a number of different covers for chairs and tables so that you can mix and match or change the mood with the seasons at the switch of a slipcover. Modern furniture suits the smart stripes and calming colour scheme – a low coffee table on wheels gives a slick look.

Accessories: A lampshade with lively horizontal stripes adds to the room's pattern power, while a metallic floor light and vase complement the cool blues. Other vases and tableware add dark accents.

LIVING ROOM TIP
When painting sharply defined stripes or checks on a wall, use low-tack masking tape to get a straight edge. It lifts off more easily than most other tapes, leaving the paintwork beneath intact

The look: Well-loved accessories and works of art can add unique personal style to a room. Here, quirky additions such as the dressmaker's dummy and doll collage say as much about the individual style of the owner as the eclectic furniture and mix of colours.

Colour: The deep lilac on the walls straddles the gap between warm and cool colours. Itself a cool hue, it harmonizes with the contemporary blues and greens, yet also gives the room a cosy feel and is rich enough to complement the more old-fashioned reds of the armchair and rug. The patterns also form an interesting mix, with the stylized flowers of the green crewelwork curtains and the crisp blue checks of the sofa alongside the traditional designs of the rug and armchair.

Fireplace: The solidly built marble fire surround gives away the room's Victorian origins and goes well with its decorative style. Its floral hearth tiles add to the diverse mix of patterns, while the wide mantelshelf makes a great display space.

Furniture: A varied mix of furniture adds to the room's individualistic charm. Each piece contributes a different style and colour – from the classic red armchair to the 1950s junk-shop cabinet with aqua-coloured doors to the contemporary lilac-painted sideboard.

Accessories: An almost childish delight in dolls and toys has provided the impetus for a collection of unusual accessories. The framed collage of brightly coloured dolls above the mantelpiece is its most striking manifestation. On the 1950s cabinet sits last year's Christmas-tree angel, while the largest 'doll' of all is the dressmaker's dummy, draped in vintage lace.

The look: This colourful room relies on hot pinks and purples for impact. Their hot, exotic quality is complemented by dark wood furniture and richly patterned cushions that add a suggestion of oriental style.

Colour: A red and purple mix is the starting point for the scheme, watered down to soft raspberry and plum. White walls lighten the look, while the roughly painted vertical band of purple adds colour without overpowering. Dark shelving, a deep red rug and a pale patterned floor cushion provide tonal variation. The timber floor works as a mid-tone against the walls.

Furniture: With the walls painted mainly in white, it's the furnishings that drive home the colour theme, and the pink sofa is its most important element. Its simple design also underlines the contemporary style of the room. The dark wood of the modular shelving unit teams well with the hot colours, and is reminiscent of oriental furniture.

Window: If your heart is set on vibrant curtains but you are afraid they might seem overwhelming, choose coloured sheers for a contemporary look. Light will filter through, toning down the strong colour and brightening the entire room. This window is also dressed with a white blind edged with a raspberry-coloured border.

Accessories: Cushions are useful tools for adding pattern and character. The gold-trimmed cover with embroidered flowers hints strongly at oriental style, while the others add to the colour mix. Vases and containers with simple shapes made from dark wood or brightly coloured glass or ceramics also add an air of eastern promise.

The look: Contemporary living often means making one space serve two or more purposes. In this open-plan room, a partition of glass bricks creates a division between the living and dining areas without compromising the feeling of light and space. It also works well with the modern decor and furniture.

Colour: In a room with a considerable floor area, its covering is important in setting the tone. Smooth light-reflective boards in a pale wood create an airy modern feel which is enhanced by the cool lilac walls and sofa. The white rug, fire surround and partition frames lighten the look further.

Partition: Glass blocks have a modern, designer feel, and look fab with sunlight shining through them. They can either be slotted into a wooden frame, as here, or used on their own to build a wall. They are available from DIY stores but, unless you're expert at DIY, it's best to get a professional to lay them as they must be reinforced for safety.

Furniture: Simple beech furniture is the perfect complement for a light, contemporary scheme. Using director's chairs with leather slings as dining seating is the ultimate in casual chic.

Fire screen: The mesh fire screen conceals a black grate, which looks incongruous amid the light atmosphere. Bend a sheet of mesh to fit your fireplace, then spray-paint it in a colour that suits your room. Do not use the screen as a fireguard as spray paint is highly flammable.

The look: Modern glamour shines from every surface in this Victorian room, where lustrous metallic paper and paint effects and jewel-coloured silks are used in a highly creative way.

Colour: A silvery sheen dominates the room, thanks to the light-reflective silver-painted floorboards. The toning wallpaper is covered with a tiny mosaic-style design that resembles a cloudy grey-green colourwash when viewed from afar. The picture rail and coving are also in silver, but the chimney breast provides a warm contrast, with its decoration of copper squares and the bright aqua and magenta fabric banner that adorns it.

Chimney breast: The wall above the marble fireplace is covered with shimmering squares of copper leaf, applied with deliberate imprecision to reveal a base coat of red paint beneath. The oriental-style banner beside them is made from hand-printed silk.

Furniture: Most of the furniture is white or light in colour and includes some distinctive pieces. Beneath its glass top, the oriental-style coffee table has a panel of white rippled sand, while a tiny drawer unit is covered in calligraphy-patterned paper.

Accessories: The decorative column is made from drum lampshades covered in jewel-coloured silks and Chinese brocades. In front of the silk banner, a potted orchid points to its oriental inspiration. Table lamps and tall candles provide pools of light to make the most of the reflective surfaces.

The look: If eye-popping colour is not your style, let texture and pattern do all the work for you. These subtle design tools can give a lift to a tranquil all-neutral scheme without overwhelming the room.

Colour and pattern: Limit your palette to natural shades such as beige, grey and cream, including a mix of light and dark tones. If you are wary of using pattern, try out the mix with cushions and throws before investing in printed upholstery or curtains – it's the cheapest way to experiment without having to live with the same designs for years. Stripes and checks are the simplest forms of patterning – stick to small-scale designs in subtle colours to prevent them overpowering the scheme.

Wall: Barely visible horizontal stripes add gentle pattern play to the wall. All the stripes are in the same paint shade but matt and gloss finishes are used alternately to enliven the plain surface. The single roll of handprinted wallpaper is a decorative feature – try this idea to add just a touch of pattern to a wall, or if a paper is too expensive to use throughout your room.

Texture: Even plain furnishings can add an element of pattern if they have attractive textures. On the sofa, fake fur, camel-hair and velvet cushions blend with a chenille throw to create their own patchwork.

Furniture: Neutral schemes reflect contemporary simplicity, so choose furniture to match. Pieces with curved lines enhance the relaxed feel, while the bamboo tray and table, woven bench and suede cube all add further textural interest.

LIVING ROOM TIP
Before you buy a sofa, especially a pale-coloured one, ask whether the fabric has been treated to resist stains. If not, buy a stainproofing spray you can apply yourself. Check that it is suitable for use on your particular upholstery material

The look: With a flowing water sculpture as its focal point, this futuristic room is designed to instil a feeling of serenity. Light colours and reflective surfaces create a sense of space, while contemporary style details update existing furniture.

Colour: Light looks lead the way for 21st-century style, so painting most of the walls white and hanging sheer muslin drapes across the large window is an easy way of achieving an atmosphere update. Wood-effect laminate flooring also gives a clean, modern look. A bright shade of aqua marks out the wall featuring the sculpture as the focal point of the room, while light-reflective metallic surfaces and accessories add hi-tech glamour.

Water sculpture: The sculpture takes the form of a dramatic 'wall of water'. The water flows down between Perspex sheets into an MDF container, made watertight with a pond liner, from where it is pumped through pipes back up to the top. Waterproof lights hidden in the base container shine up through the water.

Furniture: The dining furniture has been given a new lease of life with a coat of white paint and a sheet of metallic laminate glued on top of the table. An ugly storage heater is concealed by an MDF cover which allows hot air to circulate through its slatted front. White muslin cushions help to revive a set of 1970s leather seating.

Accessories: Plain white tableware and clear wine glasses continue the simple colour theme. The shiny tubular vase, which holds banana leaves, is made from lengths of drainpipe lined with plastic sheeting then glued to a square of MDF and sprayed with chrome-effect paint.

The look: Soothe away your cares with shades of sky and cloud to create a cool, space-enhancing colour scheme. Metallic and iridescent finishes add a silver lining.

Colour: As a cool colour, blue creates a light, airy environment, and is ideal for freshening up a stuffy room. For the best effect, use it with plenty of white. Pale muted blues give a restful feel, but using them in a lively manner produces an individual look – try choosing a number of toning shades to paint large squares on one wall. Pale wooden flooring suits the room's contemporary feel.

Wall: To chequerboard a wall, measure it and mark out a grid using chalk. Paint in your squares freehand (masking tape gives a more accurate but less characterful line). Circles and zodiac signs add extra individuality to this wall. For the circles, draw around a paint lid, or something else of a suitable size. Look for star signs in a book and copy them freehand or enlarge them on a photocopier. Trace the results onto card or acetate, and cut out to make stencils.

Furniture: Choose a simple sofa upholstered in white fabric – this one is a chair bed. Complement it with modern metallic furniture to add a silvery glimmer. A large zinc storage box doubles as a surface for stereo equipment.

Accessories: Continue the metallic touches with vases and bowls. To stop the scheme feeling too cold, add comfort with a mohair throw and a textured rug. Look for lighting to suit your scheme – a billowing white shade gives the perfect cloud effect.

LIVING ROOM TIP
When shopping for modern metal furniture, look for pieces that have a dull sheen rather than a full-on shine, as the latter will show up every scratch

The look: The style of the American Midwest comes to a Victorian living room, with a scheme featuring natural textures, cowhide prints and a huge cacti as finishing touches.

Colour: Stone-coloured paint on the walls creates a natural feel and provides a light backdrop for the warmer colours of the furniture. The window seat is painted in 'Cherokee' red, a shade favoured by Native Americans, while the sofa reflects the rich chocolate brown of the cowskin rug. The natural look continues with the wooden flooring and slate hearth tiles.

Furniture: Plenty of seating is essential for family pow-wows, so an MDF window seat has been built around the bay window. It also covers a radiator – the grille on the front allows heat through. For true prairie style, sofas should be upholstered in leather or suede.

Add extra seating with suede cubes in natural colours – to save money, make your own by covering foam blocks with fake suede. Use more suede fabric to make a herd of comfy cushions, stitching on black and white felt shapes to create a cowhide effect.

Chimney breast: With the room's battered Victorian fire surround removed, the chimney breast has been replastered into a minimal square opening. The hearth is lined with slate tiles, and an antique grate is supported by breeze blocks. On the wall above, three chunky asymmetrical shelves are coated in textured paint and edged with stained veneer.

Window: The simple white roller blinds at the bay window are decorated with a large geometric pattern, applied using black and yellow fabric paints.

The look: Green is rarely set against orange in a room, but when the two come together, stand back and watch them sizzle. They make an exotic combination, especially when they are teamed with woven furniture and a huge potted palm to give the feel of a jungle verandah.

Colour: It's important to get the balance right between the green and orange. Don't overdo them: a single orange chair and one green wall provide plenty of impact. The effect is tempered by liberal amounts of crisp white and the natural tones of the furniture and bamboo flooring. The blue curtains also help to cool things down, adding a panel of stronger colour to balance the sharp green and orange contrast. Using the colours in big blocks heightens their individual effect and gives a bold modern look.

Furniture: The contemporary curves of the orange chair contrast with the straight lines of the sofa and the birch nest tables. The basketweave sofa adds textural interest and, like the bamboo shelf unit, suggests oriental style.

Window: A curtain is useful for adding a panel of colour to break up a plain wall. If a single colour looks too strong, stitch together bands of fabric in different shades – here, a block of lighter blue mutes the effect of the darker bands. The curtain hangs from a simple bamboo rod.

Accessories: A wicker display shelf and cushions in woven and knitted fabrics add further textural interest. Oriental vases and tableware enhance the exotic atmosphere but the most evocative accessory is the enormous palm, which brings the jungle right inside.

LIVING ROOM TIP
Bamboo is an environmentally-friendly choice of wood as it grows fast and furiously. It makes superb flooring as well as furniture – the planks have a high-gloss finish and are easy to keep clean

The look: This room is designed to show off a collection of beautiful or interesting objects picked up on travels around the world. It may be tempting to complement such items with ethnic decor, but this restrained contemporary backdrop gives full glory to the exotic treasures.

Colour: A light neutral colour scheme provides a suitable blank canvas for display purposes as well as increasing the illusion of space in the tiny room. The walls are painted in a parchment shade, a softer and more sophisticated choice than bright white. The floorboards are white but covered in large rush mats which echo the warm natural textures and tones of the ethnic furniture and accessories.

Furniture: The sofas have cream covers so that they blend in with the walls without distracting attention from the smaller, more interesting pieces of furniture. These include finds from all over the globe: a Chinese rattan suitcase that doubles as a coffee table when topped with a metal tray; an oriental bamboo side table, a golden-toned Chinese trunk and an octagonal Syrian table inlaid with mother-of-pearl.

Accessories: The treasures on display are similarly eclectic in origin but they all share neutral colouring and a natural beauty that gives the room a cohesive look. Five Chinese terracotta figures are mounted on simple blocks above the sofa, while creamy vellum-covered books, ancient-looking pots and elegant horse statues all justify their place on the neat cream-coloured shelves.

LIVING ROOM TIP
Shelves with hidden battens give a streamlined look. They are available to buy, but you can also construct your own by fixing a 5 x 5cm batten to the wall and building a timber box around it. Sand the edges, then paint the box to match your walls

The look: Pungent spicy colours, comfy low seating and a soft tented ceiling – it could only be Moroccan style. If you need to bring a blast of Sahara sunshine into a chilly room, this is the look for you.

Colour: To get on course for a warm and exotic environment, think of sun-baked shades, such as sand and terracotta, and spice colours like saffron, paprika and ginger. Layer throws and cushions in a mixture of these colours, and choose a hard flooring that blends with them, such as cork or terracotta tiles. Colourful stripes on rugs and cushions also evoke the style.

Furniture: A low sofa piled with plain and patterned throws and striped cushions is an alluringly cosy focal point. Mix rough natural fabrics such as hessian and unfinished cottons with luxurious silks. In front of your sofa, place a low-level coffee table, and scatter the floor with big cushions. Look for solid dark wood furniture with carved detailing and fretwork screens made from wrought iron or wood.

Tented ceiling: Don't confine fabric drapes to the sofa – billowing swathes strung across the ceiling suggest the feel of a Bedouin tent. Vivid hessian trimmed with gold braid forms a canopy above the sofa. It is draped over a pair of dowelling rods hung from cup hooks fixed into the ceiling.

Accessories: Complete the look with decorative silver and gilt candle lanterns and oil lamps to give a romantic glow, and don't forget a Moroccan tea set with pretty coloured glasses.

The look: Lift your living room onto a spiritual plane with this atmospheric combination of pure white decor and oriental furniture. The minimalist colour scheme gives a feeling of order and peace, while allowing the beauty of the furnishings to shine.

Colour: The walls and ceiling are painted in white with an almond tint. Choosing a carpet in a similar shade to the walls will create a calming feel in any room. All-round white maximizes the sense of space, making this already large room feel fantastically bright and airy. The furniture and pot plants inject a mixture of glamour and natural tones – exotic silver, purple and orange alongside wood, terracotta and leafy greens.

Furniture: Most of this furniture is from India, and the pyramid cushions come from Thailand, but the driftwood mirror and cupboard were bought in London. You don't need to travel the world to find ethnic furniture – many high street stores now stock ranges imported from India and Asia, particularly in dark wood, bamboo and rattan. For true oriental style, choose low furniture, and pile the floor with a selection of beaded and embroidered cushions.

Window: The floaty sheers at the window continue the ethereal feel created by the white decor. They hang from a slender pole and are tied back for decorative effect with white tassels.

Accessories: Make sure light fittings suit the mood – a silvery chandelier with a large pink glass droplet suspended beneath echoes the decorative style and colours of the chairs. Add plenty of candles to aid meditation, and large potted palms for a tropical feel.

LIVING ROOM TIP
Contrast of height is as important as contrast of shape or colour in a room scheme. If you opt for mainly low-level furniture, vary the look with a few vertical features, such as tall cabinets, full-length mirrors or big plants

The look: Renowned for its cool minimalism, oriental style also has a more exotic side. This softer style mixes the best of countries from Japan through to Vietnam, with sumptuous silks and alluring pinks and purples giving a sensual boost. Add furnishings in wicker, paper and bamboo, and complete the look with crackleglaze ceramics and potted orchids.

Colour: A strong sense of colour is a key factor of this style, and pinks and purples will put passion into your room. For a livable look, combine a range of different tones, from delicate cherry blossom shades to rich plum or damson. The white woodwork and blind and the natural colours of furniture and flooring help to balance the more exotic hues.

Furniture: You may prefer a comfy Western-style sofa, but keep the oriental look alive by choosing bamboo for your other furniture. Low-level stools and tables are particularly appropriate to the Eastern style, and fashionable too – you should find a good choice in selected high-street stores. A bamboo ladder makes an unusual and elegant decorative feature.

Soft furnishings: For cushions, choose opulent-looking fabrics such as silks, satins and brocades, especially those with a glamorous sheen. Tassel trimmings and embroidered sprays of cherry blossom and orchid motifs are also in character. Choose a hardwearing weave for your sofa with an oriental motif design that fits the scheme.

Paper furnishings: The Japanese love paper, and use it in anything from flooring to screens to lampshades. This floor is covered with a woven paper mat, and the window is dressed with a paper blind.

The look: Simple living and folksy charm give the New England style of the early American settlers its enduring appeal. This refreshingly laid-back look is easy to achieve in contemporary homes using painted wooden furniture, country-style checked fabrics and rustic accessories.

Colour: Rich reds and blues combined with liberal dashes of cream is the colour recipe for this look. Use these shades as bold blocks of colour on walls, furniture and floorboards. Painted wood is particularly evocative – the lower half of this wall is covered with rustic-style panelling, highlighted by a robust red. Checked fabrics introduce pattern to balance the strong shades, while a dark blue textured rug adds colour and comfort to take the chill off the white-painted floor.

Furniture: Furniture should be simple and functional in style and made of natural materials: wooden chests of drawers provide ample storage which can be supplemented with peg rails or baskets. Sofas and armchairs can be covered with practical loose covers made from checked fabrics, to bring them into the scheme.

Soft furnishings: Checks of any kind are a key ingredient of New England style, from big bold squares to tiny ginghams. Add cushions or napkins with folk-art motifs, such as stars and hearts, to really define the look. For all soft furnishings, choose hard-wearing natural fibres such as cotton and linen.

Accessories: If you can find authentic folk-art accessories, such as the decorative wooden bird box, so much the better. Otherwise, simple bird prints and ornaments, battered tin jugs and plain earthenware bowls will all look at home on your painted furniture.

The look: Native American style has a warm, homely appeal, and with rustic wooden furniture, Navaho motifs and woven textiles you can theme your living room to create cosy surroundings fit for a chief!

Colour: To give the look a contemporary feel, keep colours to a lean palette of naturals with flashes of clear blue. In this room, walls painted in pale beige team with plain cream window treatments to create a light, simple backdrop, allowing the natural tones and textures of the furnishings to dominate. The wooden furniture, sisal floorcovering and suede cushion all add warmer colour, while the bold patterns that are vital in spelling out the look also enliven the neutral scheme.

Sofa: Bring the all-important pattern element to the fore by using a striking print to upholster your sofa – a crunchy woven fabric draped with a woollen throw gives that homely hearthside feel. Add suede or leather cushions with stitched detailing, or use tiny pieces of suede to decorate a plain cover. Beaded fringing is also a key ingredient of the Native American look.

Wooden furniture: Chunky wooden furniture that looks as if it's been hewn straight from the log will give the necessary rustic cred. Other pieces can be painted cream to blend in with the background, then jazzed up with Navaho motifs: the border stencil used to decorate the cupboard unit is repeated on the wall.

Window: Themed trimmings add character to the plainest window dressings. The cream roller blind is edged with fake suede fringing and the curtain is tied with a leather strap.

The look: Glowing colour turns up the heat in this large, high-ceilinged room, making a warm and exotic setting for ethnic statues and furniture brought back from the Far East.

Colour: The walls are covered in diluted orange paint, applied in a rough wash. Floorboards of reclaimed pine enhance the warm atmosphere, while the leather armchairs add depth with darker shades of brown. Accents of blue in the foreground armchair and the vase provide an electrifying contrast with the orange, and pink-painted pieces of paper hanging from the picture rail add alternative colour interest along one wall.

Furniture: Curvy lines characterize the shapely seating: the two squat armchairs with their gleaming polished leather and the elegant wooden couch that fills the space in front of the bay window. White cushions add a lighter touch. The coffee table – another striking shape – is the focal point of the room. Brought back from Indonesia, it is a wooden block that was once used for milling.

Accessories: Modern lamps and vases mingle happily with the more unusual pieces that give the room character. A battered old easel stands alongside two carved wooden figures, traditionally used in Thai wedding ceremonies, which flank the fireplace.

Shelving: An ingenious graduated glass and wire shelf system turns an alcove into a display area for accessories. Made by the owner of the house, it hangs from a single hook on the wall.

LIVING ROOM TIP
Applying a strong paint shade as a colourwash will give it a softer look. Start with a base coat of undiluted emulsion and leave to dry. Add water to the remaining paint until you get the strength of wash you want, then apply to the wall in crisscross strokes using a wide brush

The look: Soothing grey walls, natural textures and low furniture create a peaceful oriental-style environment. Scarlet and black beef up the look a little, and a day bed with cushions provides comfort.

Colour: Pale grey and cool cream is the ultimate chill-out combination, and the natural textures of the wooden furniture and seagrass floorcovering relax the look even further. Left at that, the room might seem lacking in energy, but it gets a lift from stimulating red and black, used sparingly in cushions and accessories.

Furniture: The furniture has been adapted to suit the scheme. The coffee table's central board has been replaced with a panel of cast concrete, which echoes the grey walls. The day bed has been converted from an ordinary bed, the headboard sawn off and concrete posts fixed to each corner. Dark wood dye deepens the colour of both pieces. A floor cushion covered in white linen and red and black cotton provides Japanese-style seating at the low table, and the day bed is covered with matching upholstery and cushions.

Radiator cover: Three pieces of chunky timber screwed together form a narrow shelf above the radiator, providing display space for books, plants and ornaments. Beneath it a cream roller blind can be lowered to hide the radiator when it is turned off.

Accessories: Tall black vases give a distinctly oriental look, as does the delicate Japanese-style scene painted in black ink on the cream wall panel. Shells scattered on the table and framed pictures of ammonites mounted above the shelf emphasize the natural theme.

The look: Bring ethnic style bang up to date by blending vibrant colours and natural textures with modern shapes. Brilliant pinks and reds inspired by Indian saris are complemented by wicker and dark-toned furniture and oriental accessories.

Colour: To keep the look contemporary, choose a wall colour that's light but not too bright. This soft mushroom shade provides a subtle foil for the earthy tones of the furniture. Raise the temperature with blocks of hot colour – for impact keep rugs and soft furnishings plain instead of going for busy ethnic patterns. This scheme combines boldly clashing pinks and reds with accents of gold.

Furniture: Straight lines and simple shapes ensure a modern feel, but look for dark-coloured furniture to suggest oriental inspiration. The wicker sofa and armchair add rugged natural texture, and are fitted with seat cushions covered in brown suede.

Soft furnishings: In a scheme where pattern is limited, it's texture and trimmings that define the ethnic look. The woven striped and pink cushions echo the texture of the sofa, while the silk bolster trimmed with gold braid gives a definite nod to glamorous sari style. Another cushion is covered in tiny mirrors edged with embroidery, also a common feature of Indian furnishings. The mirrors can be bought in packs from larger haberdashery stores, ready to sew on.

Accessories: Authentic oriental vases and containers strengthen the look, but steer clear of fussy exoticism and stick to simple shapes. They mix well with a modern woven lampshade and a striking Mark Rothko print that reflects the colours of the scheme.

The look: For a Scandinavian feel, mix a palette of beautiful blues, from duck-egg to navy, and combine them with plenty of crisp white to create a light and airy atmosphere.

Colour: Blue and white is a classic combination, yet never fails to look clean and refreshing. It is ideal for Scandinavian style, which relies on whitewashed wood and cool space-enhancing colour to brighten the gloom in northern rooms. Checks and stripes liven up the look and offer the opportunity to introduce the many shades of blue that give the scheme the tonal variation it needs. When combining checks and stripes, juxtapose designs of varied sizes to create a mix that's easy on the eye.

Furniture: Wooden furniture that's white or light is a key element of this look. Cot chairs and sofas can be made comfy with cushions that tie onto the frame. Look for tables with decorative scalloped edges which help to soften the regimented effect of the checks and stripes. If you can't find whitewashed furniture, buy ready-to-paint pieces in unfinished wood and decorate them yourself. Make mismatched chairs fit the scheme by sewing fabric covers for them.

Floor: In such a light atmosphere, whitewashed floorboards would feel a bit too chilly, but blond wood provides a natural base to offset the pale furniture. A chenille rug adds comfort underfoot.

Accessories: A large mirror and light-reflective glassware enhance the room's airiness. Other accessories stick strictly to the colour scheme, highlighting its tonal contrast with dark blue and white vases and jugs placed side by side.

LIVING ROOM TIP
If your colour scheme isn't working, it probably lacks tonal variation – a room needs a range of shades, from light to dark, to prevent it looking flat. So even if you want a perfectly pale overall effect, make sure you include one or two darker accents

STOCKISTS:

ONE-STOP SHOPS

DEBENHAMS
Furniture (catalogue only), lighting, window dressings and accessories.
Tel: 020 7408 4444
www.debenhams.com

FREEMANS
Furniture, lighting, window dressings and accessories.
Tel: 0800 900200
www.freemans.com

HABITAT
Contemporary furniture, lighting and accessories.
Tel: 0845 601 0740
www.habitat.net

HEAL'S
Contemporary furniture, fabrics, lighting and accessories.
Tel: 020 7636 1666
www.heals.co.uk

IKEA
Affordable flatpack furniture; furnishings, fabrics and lighting.
Tel: 020 8208 5600
www.ikea.co.uk

JOHN LEWIS
Wide range of furniture, fabrics, window dressings, lighting and accessories. Carpets fitted.
Tel: 020 7629 7711
www.johnlewis.co.uk

LAURA ASHLEY
Classic and country-style furniture, fabrics, window dressings, lighting and paints.
Tel: 0870 562 2116 for stockists, 0800 868100 for mail order
www.lauraashley.com

MARKS & SPENCER
Classic and modern furniture, window dressings and lighting.
Tel: 020 7935 4422 for stockists, 0845 603 1603 for mail order
www.marks-and-spencer.com

NEXT HOME
Furniture, wallpaper, paints, window dressings and lighting.
Tel: 0870 243 5435 for stockists, 0845 600 7000 for mail order
www.next.co.uk

BEAVER & TAPLEY
Freestanding modular storage
units in real wood finishes.
Tel: 0845 606 0340
www.beaverandtapley.co.uk

CARGO HOMESHOP
Sofas upholstered to order;
contemporary furniture.
Tel: 0870 0112119

THE CONRAN SHOP
Contemporary designer
furniture, furnishings and
accessories.
Tel: 020 7589 7401
www.conran.co.uk

COURTS
Sofas, sofa beds, futons and
other furniture.
Tel: 020 8640 3322
www.courts.co.uk

THE DORMY HOUSE
Wooden furniture in traditional
designs sold ready to paint.
Tel: 01264 365789
www.thedormyhouse.com

DUCAL
Solid wood furniture in classic
designs; upholstered sofas.
Tel: 01264 333666
www.ducal-furniture.co.uk

ERCOL
Solid wood furniture, including
wood-framed sofas, mainly in
traditional designs.
Tel: 01494 464488
www.ercol.com

FUTON COMPANY
Futon sofa beds and simple
Japanese-style screens.
Tel: 0845 609 4455

GRAND ILLUSIONS
French country-style wooden
furniture, painted, distressed
or waxed.
Tel: 020 8607 9446
www.maison.com

HIGHLY SPRUNG
Contemporary and traditional
sofas and sofa beds.
Tel: 020 7924 1124
www.highlysprung.co.uk

THE HOLDING COMPANY
Stylish contemporary storage
furniture and accessories.
Tel: 020 7610 9160
www.theholdingcompany.co.uk

IKINO
Modular storage systems made
from colourful plastic.
Tel: 01656 669906

IN N OUT TRADING
Oriental chests, screens and
tables in wood and iron.
Tel: 020 8452 0300
www.innout.co.uk

THE IRON DESIGN COMPANY
Handmade iron sofas, tables and
chairs. Can also make pieces to
customers' own specifications.
Tel: 01609 778143
www.irondesign.co.uk

LLOYD LOOM OF SPALDING
Woven fibre furniture, including
the classic Lloyd Loom chairs.
Tel: 01775 712111
www.lloydloom.com

THE LOOSE COVER COMPANY
Loose sofa and chair covers
made to order.
Tel: 01494 471226

MAGNET
Fitted and freestanding furniture
in a range of styles.
Branches nationwide.
www.magnet.co.uk

MCCORD DESIGN BY MAIL
Contemporary shelving units
and storage accessories.
Tel: 0870 908 7005
www.emccord.com

MARKS & SPENCER
Classic and modern furniture.
Tel: 020 7935 4422 for stockists,
0845 603 1603 for mail order
www.marks-and-spencer.com

MFI
Affordable furniture in solid
pine and other wood finishes.
Tel: 0870 241 0154
www.mfi.co.uk

MUJI
Simple contemporary shelving
units, wheeled trolleys and coffee
tables made from steel and
laminated woods.
Tel: 0870 609 5555

MULTIYORK
Custom-made sofas, sofa beds
and chairs, with thousands of
upholstery fabrics to choose
from; wooden cabinet furniture.
Tel: 0870 527 3747
www.multiyork.co.uk

OCEAN
Contemporary shelving
units and wheeled coffee
tables in beech and maple;
leather sofas.
Tel: 0870 242 6283
www.oceancatalogue.com

OKA DIRECT
Oriental-style storage units, chests and side tables in rattan and bamboo.
Tel: 0870 160 6002
www.okadirect.com

PARKER KNOLL
Sofas and upholstered furniture in generally traditional styles, plus leather ranges and cabinets
Tel: 01494 557850
www.parkerknoll.co.uk

THE PIER
Ethnic-style furniture ranges, many in dark wood or bamboo.
Tel: 020 7814 5020 for stockists, 020 7814 5004 for mail order
www.pier.co.uk

PUKKA PALACE
Colonial-style furniture made from wood and metal.
Tel: 020 7352 5674 for stockists; 0845 766 6660 for mail order
www.pukka-palace.co.uk

PURVES & PURVES
Innovative designer furniture, including chic Italian sofas and a shapely chaise longue.
Tel: 020 7580 8223 for stockists; 0870 603 0205 for mail order
www.purves.co.uk

SCUMBLE GOOSIE
Ready-to-paint wooden furniture and screens in classic designs.
Tel: 01453 731315
www.scumblegoosie.com

SHAKER
Wooden furniture mostly in cherry or maple; peg rails, oval boxes and other Shaker-style furnishings and accessories.
Tel: 020 7935 9461
www.shaker.co.uk

SOFAS AND SOFA-BEDS
Sofas and sofa beds in traditional and modern styles.
Tel: 020 7637 1932
www.sofaweb.co.uk

SOFA WORKSHOP
Wide range of sofas, including contemporary, classic and leather designs.
Tel: 01798 343400 for stockists; 01443 238699 for mailorder
www.sofaworkshopdirect.co.uk
01798 345324 for mail order
www.sofaworkshop.com

VIVA SOFA
Contemporary sofas and chairs, including leather designs.
Tel: 01443 239444
www.vivasofa.co.uk

WOOD BROS
Old Charm classic hand-carved
oak furniture; Look 2000 modern
Perspex collection.
Tel: 01920 469241
www.oldcharm.co.uk

WORLD OF LEATHER
Leather sofas and chairs,
most in contemporary styles.
worldofleather.com

FIREPLACES
AND FITTINGS

AMAZING GRATES
Reproduction period fireplaces
in marble, stone and slate.
Tel: 020 8883 9590
www.amazing-grates.co.uk

CLAYTON MUNROE
Period-style door handles.
Tel: 01803 762626
www.claytonmunroe.co.uk

ELGIN & HALL
Made-to-order fireplaces in a
wide range of styles.
Tel: 01677 450100
www.elgin.co.uk

HAF DESIGNS
Contemporary door handles in
steel and brass.
Tel: 01992 505655
www.hafdesigns.co.uk

JALI
MDF fittings made to measure,
including radiator covers,
shelving, pelmets and screens.
Tel: 01227 831710
www.jali.co.uk

KNOBS & KNOCKERS
Door furniture in modern
and traditional designs.
Tel: 020 7384 2884
www.knobsandknockers.co.uk

PECO
Vast choice of original and
reproduction doors and fully
restored fireplaces.
Tel: 020 8979 8310

RICHARD BURBIDGE
Wooden mouldings for dado
rails and panel effects.
Tel: 01691 678201
www.richardburbidge.co.uk

WICKES
Fires and fire surrounds; glass blocks for partition walls.
0870 608 9001
www.wickes.co.uk

WINTHER BROWNE
Simple fire surrounds in pine, mahogany and MDF; flatpack ready-to-paint radiator cabinets.
Tel: 020 8803 3434

PAINTS

AURO ORGANIC PAINTS
Paints and woodstains made from natural products.
Tel: 01799 543077
www.auroorganic.co.uk

B&Q
Contemporary colours, including Benetton special effects paints.
Tel: 020 7576 6502
www.diy.com

CROWN PAINTS
Vast choice, including the mix-to-order Expressions collection.
Tel: 01254 704951
www.crownpaint.co.uk

DULUX
Vast choice of shades in many ranges, including the extensive Colour Mixing System.
Tel: 01753 550555
www.dulux.co.uk

FARROW & BALL
Heritage paint shades.

Tel: 01202 876141
www.farrow-ball.co.uk

HOMEBASE
Wide choice, including ranges by Jane Churchill and Laura Ashley.
Tel: 0870 900 8098
www.homebase.co.uk

INTERNATIONAL PAINT
Paints and primers for melamine, radiators and floors.
Tel: 01962 711177
www.plascon.co.uk

SANDERSON
More than 1,000 mix-to-order colours in the Spectrum range.
Tel: 01895 830000
www.sanderson-uk.com

ZEST
Vibrant Mediterranean colours.
Tel: 020 7351 7674
www.zestessentials.com

DECORATIVE EFFECTS

CREATIVE BEADCRAFT
Wide range of beads.
Tel: 01494 715606
www.creativebeadcraft.co.uk

DYLON
Fabric dyes in many colours.
Tel: 020 8663 4296
www.dylon.co.uk

THE ENGLISH STAMP COMPANY
Wall stamps and stamping tools.
Tel: 01929 439117
www.englishstamp.com

HAMMERITE
Metallic paints and enamels for
use on iron beds or radiators.
Tel: 01661 830000
www.hammerite.com

HOMECRAFTS DIRECT
Craft products by mail order.
Tel: 0116 269 7733
www.homecrafts.co.uk

HUMBROL
Makers of Glass Etch spray that
creates a frosted effect on glass.
Tel: 01482 701191

LIBERON
Waxes and other wood finishes.
Tel: 01797 367555

THE PAINTED FINISH
Paint effects products and tools.
Tel: 01926 842376
www.craftychick.com

PÉBÉO
Fabric, china and porcelain
paints and pens.
Tel: 02380 701144
www.pebeo.com

STENCIL LIBRARY
Stencils and stencilling tools.
Tel: 01661 844844
www.stencil-library.com

SPECIALIST CRAFTS
Wide range of craft products.
Tel: 0116 269 7711 for stockists,
0116 269 7733 for mail order
www.speccrafts.co.uk

VV ROULEAUX
Ribbons, braids and trimmings.
Tel: 020 7434 3899
www.vvrouleaux.com

FABRICS AND WALLPAPERS

ANDREW MARTIN
Printed fabrics and wallpapers,
velvets, suedes and leather.
Tel: 020 7225 5100 for stockists

ANNA FRENCH
Floral and paint-effect wallpapers; printed cotton fabrics,
lace and sheers.
Tel: 020 7349 1099

CATH KIDSTON
Retro 1950s-style floral cottons.
Tel: 020 7221 4000 for stockists,
020 7229 8000 for mail order.
www.cathkidston.co.uk

COLEFAX & FOWLER
Florals on linen and chintz, and
complementary wallpapers.
Tel: 020 8877 6400

COLOROLL
Contemporary wallcoverings
and coordinating fabrics.
Tel: 0800 056 4878
www.coloroll.co.uk

**CROWN WALLCOVERINGS &
HOME FURNISHINGS**
Wide range of wallcoverings.
Tel: 0800 458 1554
www.ihdg.co.uk

DESIGNERS GUILD
Colourful contemporary fabrics,
wallpapers and paints.
Tel: 020 7351 5775
www.designersguild.com

GRAHAM & BROWN
Contemporary wallcoverings,
including textures and metallics.
Tel: 0800 3288452
www.grahambrown.com

IAN MANKIN
Natural fabrics in plains, stripes
and checks, including plenty of
classic tickings and ginghams.
Tel: 020 7722 0997

JANE CHURCHILL FABRICS
Wallpapers, cottons and linens
with floral and geometric
designs in light, contemporary
colours.
Tel: 020 8877 6400

JOHN LEWIS
Fabrics and wallpapers from
many different suppliers.
Tel: 020 7629 7711
www.johnlewis.com

KA INTERNATIONAL
Pure cottons in vibrant colours.
Tel: 020 7584 7352
www.ka-international.com

KNICKERBEAN

Discount stores with designer fabrics at bargain prices.
Tel: 01842 751327

LAURA ASHLEY

Classic and country-style fabrics and papers, especially florals.
Tel: 0870 562 2116 for stockists, 0800 868100 for mail order.
www.lauraashley.com

MALABAR

Hand-woven silks and cotton fabrics imported from India.
Tel: 020 7501 4200
www.malabar.co.uk

THE MODERN SAREE CENTRE

Sarees and Indian silks.
Tel: 020 7247 4040

THE NATURAL FABRIC COMPANY

Wide range of natural fabrics, from hessian and calico to chambray and sheers.
Tel: 01488 684002

OSBORNE & LITTLE

Classic and contemporary prints, weaves and wallpapers.
Tel: 020 7352 1456
www.osborneandlittle.com

SANDERSON

Coordinated fabric and wallcovering ranges with classic and contemporary designs.
Tel: 01895 830000
www.sanderson-uk.com

WILMAN INTERIORS

Contemporary and classic fabrics and wallpapers.
Tel: 01282 727300
www.wilman.co.uk

WINDOW TREATMENTS

AMERICAN SHUTTERS
Custom-made wooden shutters
painted or stained in the colour
of your choice.
Tel: 020 8876 5905

ARTISAN
Wide range of poles and finials,
from trendy to traditional in
style.
Tel: 01772 203555

THE CURTAIN EXCHANGE
Quality secondhand curtains
bought and sold.
Tel: 020 7731 8316
www.thecurtainexchange.cwc.net

ECLECTICS
Ready-made and made-to-
measure roller and Roman
blinds in smart modern designs.
Tel: 0870 010 2211
www.eclectics.co.uk

LUXAFLEX
Made-to-measure blinds,
including Venetians.
Tel: 08000 399399
www.luxaflex.com

PRÊT À VIVRE
Curtains and blinds made to
measure; poles and tiebacks.
Tel: 020 8960 6111
www.pretavivre.com

ROSEBYS
Ready-made curtains and blinds.
Tel: 0115 925 5999
www.rosebys.com

RUFFLETTE
Tiebacks, blind and eyelet kits
and curtain-making products.
Tel: 0161 998 1811
www.rufflette.com

THE SHUTTER SHOP
Wooden shutters made to order;
wooden Venetian blinds.
Tel: 01252 844575
www.shuttershop.co.uk

VELUX
Skylight windows and blinds
designed to fit them.
Tel: 0800 316 8822
www.velux.co.uk

FLOORING

ALLIED CARPETS
Carpet superstores with a huge range of colours and patterns.
Tel: 0800 932932

BRINTONS
Vast range of Axminster and Wilton carpets.
Tel: 0800 505055
www.brintons.co.uk

CRUCIAL TRADING
Natural floorcoverings and rugs in sisal, coir and seagrass.
Tel: 01562 825656
www.crucial-trading.com

FIRED EARTH
Tiles, wood and natural floorings and handwoven rugs.
Tel: 01295 814300
www.firedearth.com

JUNCKERS
Solid hardwood flooring in oak, beech and ash.
Tel: 01376 534705
www.junckers.dk

KÄHRS FLOORING
Hardwood flooring mostly from sustainable Swedish forests.
Tel: 01243 778747
www.kahrs.se

PERGO ORIGINAL
Wood-effect laminate flooring.
Tel: 0800 374771
www.pergo.com

THE RUG COMPANY
Handmade quality rugs from around the world.
Tel: 020 7229 5148
www.rugcompany.co.uk

RYALUX CARPETS
Plain and subtly patterned wool carpets that can be supplied in any width to avoid wastage.
Tel: 0800 163632
www.ryalux.com

TOMKINSONS CARPETS
Wide range of colours and patterns, plus jazzy borders.
Tel: 0800 374429

BHS
Stylish but affordable lights and shades in a range of styles.
Tel: 020 7262 3288
www.bhs.co.uk

CHRISTOPHER WRAY LIGHTING
Huge range of designs, from cutting-edge to traditional.
Tel: 020 7736 8434
www.christopher-wray.com

HABITAT
Modern light fittings in chrome and glass; paper shades in many shapes and sizes.
Tel: 0845 601 0740
www.habitat.net

IKEA
Contemporary designs, including very affordable table lamps.
Tel: 020 8208 5600

JOHN CULLEN LIGHTING
Discreet downlighters, spots and uplighters for creating atmospheric effects.
Tel: 020 7371 5400
www.johncullenlighting.co.uk

MATHMOS
Lava lamps in many shapes, sizes and colours.
Tel: 020 7549 2700
www.mathmos.com

MCCLOUD & CO
Vast choice of light fittings by British craftspeople, available in a selection of different finishes.
Tel: 020 7352 1533
www.mccloud.co.uk

PURVES & PURVES
Contemporary light fittings by top European designers, plus some more affordable designs.
Tel: 020 7580 8223
www.purves.co.uk

SKK LIGHTS
Innovative light fittings, including some wacky designs.
Tel: 020 7434 4095
www.skk.net

THE STIFFKEY LAMPSHOP
Original and reproduction lamps, candlesticks and candelabra.
Tel: 01328 830460

ACCESSORIES

BOMBAY DUCK
Decorative contemporary accessories, including photo frames and beaded items.
Tel: 020 8749 7000
www.bombayduck.co.uk

ELEPHANT
Varied selection of ethnic-style accessories imported from all over the world.
Tel: 020 7637 7930

FOUND
Candleholders, cushions, picture frames and other accessories, to complement both classic and contemporary looks.
Tel: 0800 316 8121
www.foundat.co.uk

THE HAMBLEDON
Stylish but practical accessories, including glass and porcelain vases, soapstone bowls and basketware.
Tel: 01962 890055

MARKS & SPENCER
Cushions, throws, vases, clocks, candleholders, photo frames and many other home accessories.
Tel: 020 7935 4422 for stockists, 0845 603 1603 for mail order
www.marks-and-spencer.com

MONSOON HOME
Embroidered throws and cushions in colourful silks.
Tel: 020 7313 3000
www.monsoon.co.uk

PAPERCHASE
Storage boxes, magazine files and desk accessories.
Tel: 020 7467 6200 for stockists; 0161 839 1500 for mail order
www.paperchase.co.uk

SIA
Wide range of small accessories designed to complement popular decorating themes.
Tel: 0870 608 6060

WAX LYRICAL
Decorative candles and candleholders.
Tel: 020 8561 0235
www.waxlyrical.co.uk

ADVICE

BRITISH BLIND & SHUTTER ASSOCIATION
Information and advice on where to buy blinds and shutters.
01827 52337
www.bbsa.co.uk

THE CARPET FOUNDATION
Free booklets giving advice on choosing and caring for carpets.
Tel: 01562 747351
www.carpetfoundation.com

THE BRITISH DECORATORS ASSOCIATION
Can supply a list of decorators in your area and a leaflet advising how to choose one.
Tel: 02476 353776

THE BUILDING CENTRE
Building information and advice; DIY guides available to buy; free reference library.
Tel: 020 7692 6200
www.buildingcentre.co.uk

THE LIGHTING ASSOCIATION
Advice on where to find answers to lighting queries; free buyers' guide available.
Tel: 01952 290905
www.lightingassociation.com

NATIONAL FIREPLACE ASSOCIATION
General information on fireplaces and fuels.
Tel: 0121 200 1310
www.nfa.org.uk

NATIONAL INSTITUTE OF CARPET AND FLOOR LAYERS
Help with finding the right professionals to fit flooring.
Tel: 0115 958 3077
www.nicsltd.org.uk

THE ROYAL INSTITUTE OF BRITISH ARCHITECTS
Can send out lists of member architects in your area.
Tel: 020 7580 5533
www.architecture.com

SALVO
Information on local salvage yards available for a small fee.
Tel: 01890 820333
www.salvo.co.uk